CONTENTS

LIST OF ABBREVIATIONS

Books by Hugh MacLennan

BR	*Barometer Rising*
CC	*Cross-Country*
EM	*Each Man's Son*
OS	*The Other Side of Hugh MacLennan*
P	*The Precipice*
RS	*Return of the Sphinx*
SR	*Scotchman's Return and Other Essays*
TT	*Thirty and Three*
TS	*Two Solitudes*
VT	*Voices in Time*
WE	*The Watch That Ends the Night*

Books by Morley Callaghan

BJ	*A Broken Journey*
CS	*Close to the Sun Again*
FP	*A Fine and Private Place*
NO	*It's Never Over*
LL	*The Loved and the Lost*
MCC	*The Many Colored Coat*
MJ	*More Joy in Heaven*
OL	*Our Lady of the Snows*
PR	*A Passion in Rome*
SF	*Strange Fugitive*
SB	*Such Is My Beloved*
TSP	*That Summer in Paris*
TSE	*They Shall Inherit the Earth*
TJ	*A Time for Judas*
WO	*A Wild Old Man on the Road*

I

A THEORETICAL INTRODUCTION:
FAITH AND FICTION

1. The Problem of Faith

We live in a post-Christian era. The legacy of the twentieth century was the death of God in the nineteenth century. Charles Darwin's *The Origin of Species* (1859) undermined the Christian concept of humanity created in the image of God with special rights and privileges, reducing it to an element in the order of Nature, red in tooth and claw, subject to evolutionary laws. Feuerback explained away God as a projection of humanity's own infinite desires, and Marx suggested that religious ideologies were an attempt to escape social oppression. Nietzsche's announcement that "God is dead" simply recognized that with the destruction of the traditional theistic idea of God went all the ethical values and meanings of the past.

Without the dimension of a personal and infinite God, the world becomes an insensitive and mechanical universe, indifferent to human goals and aspirations, seemingly without ultimate meaning or purpose. Moreover, in an age of the Holocaust and Hiroshima, humanity has lost its former faith in rationalism, science, and humanism. These concerns gave rise to existentialism, the dominant philosophy for most of the twentieth century.

Existentialism is "a philosophy dedicated to the proposition that man is doomed but not damned": free from guilt but doomed to death in a universe without absolute moral or spiritual values (Glicksberg 7). The result is existential alienation, despair, and angst, or anxiety, in a world of ultimate meaninglessness. Only by individually acknowledging and taking upon oneself the anxiety of finitude and emptiness can one affirm one's existence and create one's own meaning. Quoting Jean Paul Sartre, "the essence of man is his existence," the theologian Paul Tillich calls this existential affirmation "the courage of despair" which has produced the brilliant modern art of Sartre, Camus, Kafka, and Beckett. The problem is that this creative act so often degenerates into nihilistic cynicism: "no belief in reason, no criterion of truth, no set of values, no answer to the question of meaning" (Tillich, *Courage* 145-48). Moreover, this philosophy does not satisfy the metaphysical craving, the spiritual element and search for ultimate purpose, that seems to be endemic in humanity. Numerous modern literary critics, such as Charles Glicksberg, have pointed out the limitations of a view of humanity that fails to do justice to its religious aspirations:

> For there is in man a vertical as well as horizontal dynamism, an upward reach of vision, an existential involvement in becoming, a craving not to be denied for transcendence. But how can he possibly fulfil this craving in a universe that has been stripped of the supernatural? (Glicksberg 9)

Both theologians and religious writers have attempted to respond to the need for spirituality in an age bereft of God. In Western culture, Protestants and Roman Catholics have reacted in different ways to the demand for a "theology of mediation" in the conflict between the religious tradition and the modern mind. The main difference between Roman Catholic and Protestant theology lies in their concepts of the relationship between God and humanity. Although both would agree that mankind is separated from God by an "infinite qualitative difference" (Reinhardt 5), the Reformers (heirs of Augustine and therefore Plato) emphasize God as "wholly Other" from whom humanity is removed by the immeasurable gulf of human sinfulness, which is bridged only by the unmerited gift of God's grace. Roman Catholicism, however, in the tradition of Thomas Aquinas and thence Aristotle, has stressed God's "Otherness" in mystical union with humanity through the Incarnation and immanent in His world.

Protestantism, therefore, has always maintained an uneasy alliance between the two ways of knowing God: "natural" or "rational theology," which begins with empirical and rational arguments for the existence of God, and "supernatural" or "revealed theology," which is based on sources of revelation — for Protestants almost exclusively the authority of the Bible. Catholicism, on the other hand, balances rational theology with revelation that includes the developing traditions of the church. The battle of scripture versus ecclesiastical tradition was, of course, fought in the Reformation. But during the Enlightenment rational theology began to struggle against revealed theology, claiming that the Scriptures were no longer infallible and stressing the "subjective" element of "existential participation" in human experience of God. This schism has grown, despite the efforts of nineteenth- and twentieth-century theologians, until we arrive at the universal breakdown of belief in the twentieth century (Tillich, *Perspectives* 14-23).

Modern Protestant theology, therefore, in attempting to respond to the spiritual crisis of our era, has split into its two main constitutive streams of "revealed" and "natural" theology. The neo-orthodox theologians, such as Karl Barth, advocate a return to the Reformers' emphasis on revelation, the theology of the Word of God. In contrast, liberal theologians, like Paul Tillich, deny the relevance of past dogma in a post-Nietzschean world and repudiate orthodox concepts of God: "This is the God Nietzsche said had to be killed. . . ." Tillich redefines God for this century, based on "existential experience," as the "God above the God of theism," "the ground of being," and the answer to modern doubts and the existential quest for meaning, the source of the "courage to be" (Tillich, *Courage* 179-83).

Roman Catholicism has often seemed much more stable and secure than the Reformers' fiery faith:

> The contemporary Roman Catholic had until recently lived essentially in the religious and cultural climate created by the Counter-Reformation and the Council of Trent. He had come to regard himself in a fixed relationship to God and to the world and had come to see in the supernatural order a guarantee of his security in the world, in his family and in himself. (Reinhardt 22)

However, in the spiritual crisis of contemporary society and the theological ferments after the Second World War and especially since Vatican II, Catholics no longer enjoy a complacent spiritual existence. With confrontation between progressive and reactionary elements, "Catholicism has been agitated by the problem of how far change would go." Some Catholic theologians have called for a more "empirical" and "inductive" theology, based on personal "experience," that is analogous to Tillich's natural theology (Dooley, "Catching" 251-53). The denominational ghettos created over the centuries had produced, in many cases, dogmatic conformists not saints. Now they have been challenged by the forces of Catholic renewal (for example, the French neo-Thomist theologian, Jacques Maritain, whose *Integral Humanism* we will explore in Part 2). Kurt Reinhardt discusses "some of the French writers of the *renouveau catholique* . . . [who] have made a distinction between the 'protected' and the 'exposed' Christian":

> Thus the living faith of the "exposed" Christian, a faith that finds itself challenged again and again, has a deeper understanding of the non-believer than the smug and self-assured "Christian," whose "faith" can hardly be distinguished from indifference. (Reinhardt 24-25)

Both Protestants and Catholics are today stressing the importance of the existential participation of Christians in the world and the Body of Christ. And many would agree with the Christian existentialist philosopher Karl Jaspers that "God is encountered in the 'limit-situations' of human existence (sin, guilt, strife, suffering, death)" (Reinhardt 29). Therefore, Christians must participate in and share the concerns of those crisis situations in order to communicate God to a godless world, to mediate, as Paul Tillich says, between theology and culture (Tillich, *Theology of Culture* 207-8).

2. The Problem of Fiction

The spiritual crisis of our century and the Christian theological responses to it form a crucial backdrop to any discussion of modern literature and religion. It has been said, by authors and literary critics as well as theologians, that all literature is essentially religious:

> Whatever the subject matter which an artist chooses, however strong or weak his artistic form, he cannot help but betray by his style his own ultimate concern, as well as that of his group, and his period. He cannot escape religion even if he rejects religion, for religion is the state of being ultimately concerned. (Tillich, *Theology of Culture* 70)

Such a broad definition of "religious" (sometimes called "metaphysics of literature") has led to some very interesting explorations of non-theological writers, such as Sartre, Camus, Kafka, Beckett, Conrad, Lawrence, Faulkner, and Hemingway.[1] My study, however, falls into the category of more "traditional" theological criticism (Gunn 35-36), concerned with those relatively few modern writers who "overtly deal with a publicly recognized presence of the divine" (Hanna 85), for example, Greene, Waugh, Mauriac, O'Connor, Percy, and Updike.[2] These novelists foreground the presence of the eternal in the temporal and privilege the relationship of their characters to God (variously and tentatively defined) as the determining factor in their existential search for meaning. I am not concerned with the "religious novel" as that minor genre written for the encouragement of the faithful, but with the problems and solutions of dramatizing a religious vision in the modern realistic novel written for an audience of nonbelievers. My study, which, I hope, has "no theological axe to grind, which [was] conceived, researched, and composed with the sole purpose of attempting to mediate the relationship between text and context . . ." (Gunn 36), centres on the work of two unorthodox but clearly theistic Canadian writers, Hugh MacLennan and Morley Callaghan; it is, I believe, the first of its kind in Canadian literary criticism.

I agree with T. R. Wright that the realistic novel has been constructed as empirical, anti-metaphysical, and implicitly ideological — in the twentieth century predominantly a product of a liberal humanist discourse.

> The novel is generally regarded as the most "realistic" of literary genres but what is actually meant by this term tends to vary. First used in the mid-nineteenth century, when the Pre-Raphaelites were demanding in painting a meticulous attention to detail, realism involved for Zola the refusal to omit what others regarded as morbid or disgusting. For Auerbach it meant the serious treatment of mundane subjects, for Lukács the depiction of the world as it really was. "Real," for the positivists, was synonymous with "certain," "precise," empirically verifiable, necessarily excluding any theological or metaphysical abstractions. Many of the major realist novelists, most notably

George Eliot, have been positivists, committed to explaining in scientific terms how it is that "superstitious" people come to believe in the "supernatural." (Wright 110)

Wright quotes Georg Lukács's *The Theory of the Novel*: "The novel is the epic of a world that has been abandoned by God" (Wright 110-11). Some modern religious novelists, however, have resisted this supposedly rational and transparent representation of reality, opposing the humanist ideology with a theology that insists on "the 'reality' of the supernatural" and challenges readers "to abandon the secular assumptions of their age" (Wright 121).

Flannery O'Connor, one of the finest religious writers of our century, expressed her frustration at the problem of communicating faith in fiction in her best-known essay, "Novelist and Believer":

> The problem of the novelist who wishes to write about man's encounter with this God is how he shall make the experience — which is both natural and supernatural — understandable, and credible, to his reader. In any age this would be a problem, but in our own, it is a well-nigh insurmountable one. Today's audience is one in which religious feeling has become, if not atrophied, at least vaporous and sentimental. (71)

She concludes that:

> I don't believe that we shall have great religious fiction until we have again that happy combination of believing artist and believing society. Until that time, the novelist will have to do the best he can in travail with the world he has. He may find in the end that instead of reflecting the image at the heart of things, he has only reflected our broken condition and, through it, the face of the devil we are possessed by. (74-75)

O'Connor's final words demonstrate the connection between contemporary religious poetics and the contemporary theological debates I have outlined. In simplified terms, the religious novelist's dilemma resolves itself into two possibilities: does she offer a dogmatic answer imposed from the outside onto her characters' struggles for meaning ("revealed theology" — "the image at the heart of things"), or can she only realize an imaginative solution arising out of the existential experience of her characters ("natural theology" — "our broken condition")?

Some literary critics have resolved the paradoxical tension inherent within the concept of the "religious novel" by denying that the genre even exists. Charles Glicksberg says: "There are no religious novels *per se*." The religious novelist may posit religion as the whole of life, God as the solution to all finite problems, and faith as the answer to evil and suffering, "but the art of fiction perversely resists his efforts to communicate the fullness of this vision. . . . Art, in short, abhors dogma" (71-72). Similarly, Murray Krieger, while allowing that a Christian writer may perceive a deeper reality in God who resolves all existential absurdities, denies that this "leap" of faith is artistically valid "since it cannot be communicated or subjected to dramatic portrayal" (265-66). Nevertheless, Glicksberg goes on to say that "there are novels that are profoundly religious in content without ceasing to be novels," and he cites the universal appeal of the Catholic novelists Graham Greene and François Mauriac. How have these writers overcome the paradoxes of a Christian aesthetic?

> In their works, religion is presented as experience, as spiritual conflict, as vision and aspiration, struggle and search and suffering, not as codified theology. What we get is a convincing and comprehensive picture of life in all its irreducible mysteriousness. (72)

We have returned, therefore, to the analogy of revealed ("codified theology") versus natural ("experience") theology. Religious novelists, as novelists, must have as strong a commitment to their art as to their faith. As we have seen, the novel has been constructed as a "realistic" genre, a mimesis of secular life. This theoretical premise has caused some of the most prominent modern Christian writers (for example, C. S. Lewis and J. R. R. Tolkien[3]) to abandon the novel in favour of theological fantasies. Religious novelists, however, who choose to incarnate the supernatural in the natural cannot deny or distort the latter. Their "existential participation" in the "limit-situations" of their readers means admitting evil, suffering, disbelief, and temptation — in other words "sin" — into their fictional worlds along with righteousness and belief. They must honestly portray the agonies of doubt along with the fervours of faith. Above all, they cannot impose a supernatural solution on the existential struggles of their characters *deus ex machina*, nor miraculously transpose their finite quests into an infinite realm. Therefore, the struggle for religious meaning against doubt and sin cannot be expounded as abstract dogma, but must be integrated into the fabric of the plot, presented as dramatic conflict arising out of the convictions of the characters, and resolved with fidelity to the artistic logic of the fiction and the finite complexities of life.

Before I consider the strategies and successes (or failures) of two Canadian religious writers, I would like to pose as a paradigm the struggle between faith and fiction in the works of Graham Greene and François Mauriac who, in prominence and production, are the foremost religious novelists of the twentieth century. Philip Stratford, in a perceptive study of their creative processes, has suggested that it is the "tension which results from this unresolved conflict" between "artistic aims and religious beliefs" which gives their work a "singularity and distinction" that appeals to both believers and non-believers (xi). Pragmatically unorthodox when necessary, Greene, like Mauriac, thought of himself, using Newman's distinction, as "a Catholic who was a novelist, not a Catholic novelist" (qtd. in Stratford 289). Their novels, whether treating overtly "Catholic" themes or more secular material, display not theological abstractions but (in Mauriac's term) metaphysics worked in concrete. As they make incarnate not only grace but the fallen nature of sin and evil, their motto could well be the quotation from Péguy that Greene used as the epigraph to *The Heart of the Matter*: "The sinner is at the very heart of Christianity. . . . None is so competent in matters of Christianity. None, if it is not the saint" (qtd. in Stratford 24). Their portrayals of the prodigal, the outcast, and the atheist reflect (as Mauriac said of *The Knot of Vipers*) their belief that Christ "came to seek out and save that which was lost" (qtd. in Stratford 193). In the struggle between good and evil, they demonstrate "the use made of sin by Grace" (Mauriac's description of *The Power and the Glory*) and "the . . . appalling . . . strangeness of the mercy of God" (the theme from *Brighton Rock*) (both qtd. in Stratford 197 and 193).

The Christian novelist who wishes to communicate a natural theology to a post-Christian society must dramatize the existential action of God's grace in fallen nature. The constant problem for any novelist — balancing freedom of character development against authorial control of the plot — is greatly magnified when the novelist's theme is the intervention of the supernatural into the natural. Stratford says that the solution for Greene and Mauriac was to attempt to make their novels "character-centred" and allow these characters free will to develop according to their own interior artistic logic. The relation between novelist and character is really analogous to the theological paradox of divine omniscience and human liberty; the novelist's respect for the individuality and mystery of his characters gives them a spiritual dimension (228). Therefore, the authors' "Christ-like identification" (220) with their characters, "their own effort of understanding and compassion, corresponds to Grace working to redeem their fallen characters" (217).

This artistic compassion, however, also has the heretical pitfalls which are the potential distortions of natural theology: Manichaeism and Jansenism. Greene tends to glamorize evil, and Mauriac sometimes makes his sinners seem like helpless victims. The problem of maintaining a balance between existential compassion and theological judgement is that grace may degenerate into a vast indulgence which is not salvation. Mauriac articulated the conflict between nature and grace that is at the core of all religious fiction: "How can I reconcile so distorted a view of the human animal with the faith I claim to have in his vocation to sanctity?" (qtd. in Stratford 304-5). In the end he could not, and, like Greene, he stopped writing Catholic novels.

The religious novel, then, is a theoretical paradox. Even if critics and novelists seem to agree on what I have termed "natural theology" as the most promising approach to content, how can sacred language be embodied in a secular text? T. S. Eliot complained about the loss of universal religious symbols at mid-century:

> Much has been said everywhere about the decline of religious belief; not so much notice has been taken of the decline of religious sensibility. The trouble of the modern age is not merely the inability to believe certain things about God and man which our forefathers believed, but the inability to *feel* towards God and man as they did. A belief in which you no longer believe is something which to some extent you can still understand; but when religious feeling disappears, the words in which men have struggled to express it become meaningless. (*On Poetry* 25)

Brian Wicker maintains that metaphor is impossible without a metaphysics, a "vertical axis" which is the religious worldview (194). Not surprisingly, the realistic novel is, in contrast, essentially metonymic.

Again, the difference between Protestant and Roman Catholic theologies may be relevant to this problem and may provide some explanation for the fact that virtually all of the best religious novelists of this century have been Catholic. Flannery O'Connor notes that "the real novelist knows that he cannot approach the infinite directly, that he must penetrate the natural human world as it is. The more sacramental his theology, . . ." the more easily he can incarnate "the supernatural" in the natural (72). As Amos Wilder points out, "The Roman doctrine of transubstantiation in the Mass is the key to Catholic art. It defines the relation of grace to nature, and the relations of the Catholic artist to the world" (85-86). As we shall see in Callaghan's works, even the least philosophical of Catholic writers realizes that, by embodying divine significance in earthly objects, this sacramental theology establishes the basis for symbolism and the metaphoric use of language.[4]

In contrast, as the Anglican critic, Malcolm Ross, has complained: "Protestant theology rejected the doctrine of transubstantiation, denied the 'real presence,' and allegedly cut off the created world, so that it could no longer be a valid bearer of the divine meaning" (qtd. in Wilder 86-87). Protestant writers inherit a dualistic theology that privileges the Word but often separates it from the word. The dangers of a Protestant aesthetic, therefore, are twofold: a vaporous spirituality that rejects the natural world as "fallen" and therefore unworthy of God's grace; and, on the other hand, a subjective, individualistic apprehension of revelation and redemption that is incommunicable to a wider audience. We will find both of these tendencies in MacLennan's fiction.

3. Faith and Canadian Fiction: MacLennan and Callaghan

In my application of theological criticism to Canadian fiction, I hope to illuminate, in a way not previously practised, the theological premises and literary productions of the two most important and influential Canadian novelists before 1960: Hugh MacLennan and Morley Callaghan. This is not primarily a comparative study, but I will suggest some contrasts between their faith and fiction in this introduction. There is no indication of any direct literary influence between the two great contemporaries; their temperaments, traditions, and techniques were very different. Nevertheless, they were both religious novelists during the period when Canada and Canadian writing entered a non-religious modern era, and, whether as models or cautions, they influenced the development of our culture.

In analyzing the connections between theology and literature in these writers and the strengths and weaknesses of their religious novels, my focus and criteria will not be theological but literary. Bad dogma can make good art; orthodox theology is no guarantee of literary success. Rather, the measure will have to be the authenticity and efficacy of their fiction. In this approach, I follow Mauriac's creed:

> A good critic, in my view, is one who, rather than expect a writer to be something other than he is, will try to discover in his works whether he has been faithful to the laws of his own universe, whether he has relied only on his own natural gifts, whether he has avoided falling back on certain formulas and certain fads. (qtd. in Stratford xii)

As we shall see in Part I, Hugh MacLennan characterized his personal spiritual struggles as typical of his generation. His own journey from Calvinism to Christian existentialism is documented in his essays and fictionalized in his novels. MacLennan's solution to the problem of writing a religious novel in a post-Christian society is a redefinition of God to answer the modern questions about meaning and purpose within the existential situation of his characters. His emphasis on natural theology indicates striking affinities with the liberal Protestantism most commonly associated with Paul Tillich.

MacLennan's theology betrays its Protestant-Augustinian heritage of Platonic dualism in its polarity of idealism and subjectivism. His "new vision of God" is a philosophical and hypothetical synthesis of science and mysticism. God is also, however, no longer a Person with an objective reality independent of the individual's subjective perception of Him. A relationship with this transcendent, impersonal deity is difficult to communicate dramatically. Therefore, despite MacLennan's "existential participation" in the "limit-situations" of his characters, his theological answers sometimes seem arbitrarily and dogmatically "revealed."

For most of his life, MacLennan was an academic and essayist, by temperament and vocation committed to instructing the public and providing solutions to the cultural and social problems of his time. His religious perspective was a dominant part of that larger worldview of history and sociology — particularly concerning the development of Canadian identity — that determined all of his novels. MacLennan's well-known didacticism, however, was also a product of his Protestantism, a theology that privileges the preaching of Scripture above all sacraments (and results in the long Presbyterian sermons that MacLennan heard every Sunday in his youth). This primacy of the Word as the source of grace led MacLennan to the opposite narrative strategy from that of Greene and Mauriac: his novels are usually thesis-centred rather than character-centred.

A theological tendency to view the Word as invoked rather than embodied may explain, therefore, some of the weaknesses which critics have noted in MacLennan's fictions. His plot structures are often schematically contrived; the endings seem to be thematically predestined and externally invoked. His major characters are not the "sinners" common to Greene, Mauriac, O'Connor, and Callaghan, but are variations on repeated mythological and romantic archetypes. They frequently function as vehicles for his ideas and spokespersons for his sermons — even as puppets of a deterministic God. Moreover, while MacLennan's symbolism is intellectually powerful, it is, again, scriptural rather than sacramental, extrinsic rather than incarnate. There are a few key tropes in every novel, but they are artificially imposed and allegorically defined by the philosophical pattern of the narrative.[5]

MacLennan's strengths, however, are also numerous and also partly the product of his theology. Protestantism has endowed the individual soul and the secular vocation of humanity with the kind of value and dignity that traditional Catholicism often reserves only for the ecclesiastical and the sacred. Consequently, MacLennan's view of life is not characterized by "post-modern" nihilism or absurdity but by an ultimate spiritual optimism for humanity. His commitment to the enlightenment and redemption of his world is shown in a compassion for his characters, a respect for human action, and a detailed evocation of setting that expresses his great love for his country.

These two foremost Canadian novelists of mid-century share so many similarities in age, gender, race, education, status, and even (during their adult lives) geography, that it is perhaps surprising that their literary works are distinguished mainly by differences. In terms of the religious novel, many of these contrasts arise from their personal theologies. MacLennan began with a loss of faith and a belief in humanism and journeyed toward a liberal Protestantism to counter the humanistic disillusionment of his generation. In contrast, Callaghan, a cradle Catholic with an instinctive sense of original sin, was influenced by Christian personalism and seems to have developed more faith in the capacity of human love to redeem the times.

More intuitively and less intellectually than MacLennan, Callaghan immersed himself in the struggles of his characters against "sin, the world, and the devil" and toward grace and redemption. His religious vision of the sacred incarnate in the secular was a product of his Catholic heritage (neo-Thomist and therefore indebted to Aristotle) which balanced transcendence with immanence in the doctrines of the incarnation and transubstantiation.

However, his solution to the paradox of the religious novel was more particularly indebted to the Christian humanism or personalism of Catholic philosopher, Jacques Maritain.

This Catholic brand of "natural theology" gave Callaghan a perspective that was neither naturalistic nor dualistic. In his best novels, he dramatizes, as Maritain recommends, the struggle to realize the Gospel virtues in the socio-economic realities of this world. Therefore, Callaghan's "existential participation" in the "limit-situations" of his characters results, not so much in dogmatic revelations like MacLennan's, but in ambiguous intimations of grace operating in nature.

While I have speculated that MacLennan began his novels with a thesis and a didactic impulse, Callaghan, by virtue of both temperament and theology, seems to have begun his novels with a character, or, as one critic says: "a strong sense of a certain kind of person whose destiny is as yet not fully defined; the 'subject' is, what will he or she 'do'?" (Watt, "Callaghan's *Passion*" 85). This decision to allow his characters to determine his plots produces "character-centred" novels similar to those of Greene and Mauriac. Like them, Callaghan displays a "Christ-like" identification with and compassion for his characters in their existential situations.

However, Maritain's incarnational humanism also gave Callaghan a respect, not only for his characters' sufferings, but for their "creative forces" (*Integral* 2): their reason, free will, dignity, and potential for personal freedom and spiritual grace. Consequently, Callaghan differs strongly from Greene and Mauriac in what he calls their Jansenist or Albigensian heresies (Weaver 25-26), a dualism that, according to him, results in a "disgust with the flesh born of an alleged awareness of an approaching doomsday" (*TSP* 95). For Callaghan, too, "the sinner is at the very heart of Christianity," and he frequently confuses him or her with the saint. More than MacLennan, he portrays the sordid and pathetic aspects of life. Yet his sinners are not all helpless victims; his view is neither morbid nor dreary (his criticisms of Greene and Mauriac). The promise of Christian humanism, that "the world is saved in hope, and the blood of Christ, the vivifying principle of the redemption, acts already within it" (*Integral* 126), gives Callaghan a muted spiritual optimism, not unlike MacLennan's, but, in his best novels, more intrinsic than didactic.

These virtues, however, also lead Callaghan to his greatest weakness, which also seems to have been an occupational hazard for Catholic writers such as Greene and Mauriac. Callaghan's compassionate understanding of and involvement in the existential struggles of his characters, and the freedom he allows them to determine their fates, can result in "a certain moral flabbiness." Rather than "a firm philosophy, a clearly articulated sense of values, . . . Callaghan invites us merely to a feast of pity" (Pacey, *Creative* 211). This defect is the opposite of MacLennan's didacticism. However, Callaghan was never an academic, an intellectual, an essayist — or a Protestant. Like O'Connor, he faithfully portrays "our broken condition . . . the face of the devil we are possessed by." And in his best novels he also reflects "the image at the heart of things" (74-75), resolving the tension between faith and fiction through a sacramental union of the supernatural and the natural. In his later works, however, the difficulties of defining the action of grace in nature seem to have defeated him, and his novels become flabbier in form and meaning.

Callaghan's style is similarly dichotomous and intentionally theological. It has been both praised and savaged.[6] Never a post-modern, Callaghan asserted a moral and mimetic function for his use of language: to "tell the truth cleanly" in words "as transparent as glass," avoiding fraudulence and distortion (*TSP* 20-21). This "gay celebration of things as they were" aimed for the incarnate rather than the idealistic; his "happy acceptance of reality" was grounded in sacramental theology: "the word made flesh" (*TSP* 148). Therefore, although he denounced "the escape into metaphor" (*TSP* 20), symbols abound in his novels. In his best works, they are concrete universals (in contrast to MacLennan's allegorical indicators), fusing the noumenal with the phenomenal. In his worst novels, they are either blatantly obtrusive or confusingly obscure. His style, too, varies from movingly transparent and truthful, to simply monotonous and pedestrian.

Hugh MacLennan and Morley Callaghan struggled with the tensions between faith and fiction from differing theological perspectives, and their religious visions contributed to their very different literary productions and the strengths and weaknesses of their art. A literary analysis that reveals the theological patterns and developments in their works will, I hope, illuminate some new aspects of these "canonical" Canadian religious novels.

Notes

[1] See, for example, in *Works Cited*, books by Charles Glicksberg, Murray Krieger, George Panichas, and G. B. Tennyson and Edward E. Ericson, Jr.

[2] See, for example, in *Works Cited*, books by Philip Stratford, Peter Hawkins, and Robert Detweiler.

[3] See, for example, C. S. Lewis, "On Science Fiction," in *Of Other Worlds*, ed. W. Hooper (New York: Harcourt Brace Jovanovitch, 1972), 59-73; and J. R. R. Tolkien, "On Fairy Tales," in *Tree and Leaf* (Boston: Houghton-Mifflin, 1965), 3-73.

[4] For example, as we shall see, Morley Callaghan disparages literary language and metaphor but in *That Summer in Paris* espouses an aesthetic based on sacramental theology: "the word made flesh" (148). More philosophically, the Canadian Catholic novelist Hugh Hood in "The Absolute Infant" and "The Ontology of Super-realism" outlines the sacramental basis for Catholic art in neo-Thomist theology indebted to Aristotelian hylomorphism (the unity of form and matter): "all things . . . are rich, full of splendour, the radiance of their formal perfection given to them by the fact of the incarnation. Everything is full of God"

("Absolute" 144). Therefore, he attempts to demonstrate in his works "the transcendental element dwelling in living things" ("Ontology" 130).

[5] The tradition of Protestant allegory is, of course, profoundly theological as evidenced in Spenser, Bunyan, and Swift, and, according to some critics, differs from Roman Catholic allegory precisely in its extrinsic nature:

> I distinguish between two basic kinds of allegory from the time of Boethius on. One of them is what I would think of as Roman Catholic notions of Christian allegory, and the other is more Reformist and Northern and English. Thinking in critical shorthand, I'd say Dantean allegory and Spenserian allegory. I think there are major differences, I mean quite serious and rooted differences, between them. I think that Dantean allegory is very much more able to save the world, and to preserve this world, than Spenserian. I don't feel the same commitment to this world in Spenserian allegory that I do in Dantean. I tend to find Spenser dualistic and Platonist and to have not as substantial an awareness of the fleshly solidity of things. (Hugh Hood, "An Interview" with J. R. (Tim) Struthers, *Essays on Canadian Writing* 13/14 (1978-79): 49)

[6] See John Metcalf, "Winner Take All," in *Essays on Canadian Writing* 51/52 (1993-94): 113-45.

II

HUGH MACLENNAN

1. Introduction

Hugh MacLennan, one of the founding fathers of modern Canadian fiction, was also the self-appointed spokesman for Canada in the twentieth century. From 1907 to 1990 he witnessed most of the extreme political, social, and religious upheavals of this turbulent century. In six books of essays and seven novels he chronicled his historical and sociological view of the maturation of our country from colonial optimism to atomic angst and paralleled it with his own personal spiritual journey from Calvinism to Christian existentialism. MacLennan's perspective was radically determined by his religious concerns. In this post-Christian society he still concentrated on the importance of the human spirit as the mediator between the existential human condition and what he still perceived as "the will of God":

> I use this latter word with apology and sometimes think it should be retired from the language; it has been so debased that the people who use it seldom know themselves what they mean. . . . But what is truth? What is the purpose of life? What is God's will? — what matters here is not that these questions can never be adequately answered. What matters is that they must be *asked* if a society is to survive. (*SR* 75)

MacLennan's socio-religious perspective was personal rather than profound. It was a product of his own struggle against a repressive religious upbringing and of his quest for a theological alternative. Furthermore, he generalized from his private spiritual development to what he considered a typical pattern of modern religious experience. He discussed these religious concerns explicitly in his many essays, and his didactic interest in modern spirituality strongly conditioned the themes and forms of his fiction.

We can trace MacLennan's own religious odyssey through his essays, remembering that, although he was an intelligent and well-trained historian, his public pronouncements were coloured by his personal experience. He says he was raised in strict Presbyterian Calvinism in a time and place "in which people were conscious of religion" (*CC* 136). But the advances of science and the disillusionment of two world wars and the Depression caused such a "fracture with two thousand years of religious tradition" (*CC* 135) that by the late 1940s Protestant North America had "largely become a pagan civilization" (*CC* 137).   MacLennan's point, based on his own loss of traditional faith, is that we live in a "post-Christian era" (*OS* 280).

MacLennan justly identifies Presbyterianism, the denomination, with Calvinism, the theological doctrine it professes. However, he further equates the Calvinist religion with a joyless, repressed "puritan" mentality; this view is probably a result of his particular upbringing as well as being a popular modern misconception. In any case he believes Canadian society has been conditioned from the beginning by Calvinist forces (both Protestant and Roman Catholic Jansenist), and puritanism as a psychology has prevailed long after the waning of established religion, enormously inhibiting the Canadian character in the process (*CC* 8). In his works MacLennan generalizes his personal rebellion against this "pernicious doctrine" into a metaphor for the Canadian experience. He claims that puritanism has taken different forms in Canada and the United States: "Americans are proud of what they do. The excessive puritanism of Canadians makes them proud of what they don't do" (*CC* 53-54). But the Calvinist puritanical legacy is a "futile, haunting, primitive sense of guilt" (*CC* 139) that has distorted life, degraded sex, devalued aesthetics, and destroyed the creative spirit through the god of materialism (*TT* 127, 216). Salvation by works, "the puritan conception that what a man does can be separated from what a man is," has become the rationale for mass production, North American affluence, and, ironically, for the very unchristian doctrine "that the production, acquisition and distribution of material goods is the final purpose of human life" (*CC* 93-94).

In his essays MacLennan denounces puritanism and its "old taboo-morality of Augustine and Calvin" ("Defence" 23). However, he also fears the rebellion leading to its logical antithesis, a sexual licence more decadent than that of the late Roman Empire; "instead of seeking a true idea of the Divine Power, it seemed easier to get rid of God entirely. With God out of the way, you could have all the sex you were capable of" (*OS* 282). He warns: "History reveals clearly that no civilization has long survived after that civilization has lost its religion" (*CC* 140). Moreover, if "the state of mind resulting from our loss of the sense of God's nearness constitutes the greatest crisis of our time" (*CC* 143), this loss of faith is due to the dominance of science and rationalism in our society. And the *apparent* incompatibility of science and religion within the modern mind he again ascribes to the evils of a "puritan education" which exchanges mysticism for materialism (*CC* 153):

So the end-product of puritanism has been enthroned, science unreconciled with religion, and by what seem to be logical steps we have been led into the solitude of a purposeless universe. This is what I believe to be the essence of the spiritual crisis we face. We are alone and we are purposeless. (*CC* 154)

However, since "where religion is concerned nature abhors a vacuum," God was replaced by those aberrations of the religious impulse, "Nationalism, Fascism and Communism" (*CC* 141), and "the worship of collective humanity" which "has had appalling consequences for human self-respect and sanity" (*OS* 282). MacLennan has said that he, like many of his contemporaries, briefly found an alternative god among these political and social systems of the thirties, and a deceptive peace as a liberal intellectual in the affluent society of the fifties. But he feels his idealistic generation achieved neither personal nor social salvation but only spiritual bankruptcy.

However, MacLennan feels that now "with the churches all but empty shells, the hunger for a believable religion may well be stronger than at any time in world history since the reign of Caracalla" (*CC* xviii). And he does not believe that traditional Christian doctrine contains "a countervailing idea great enough and sustaining enough to save society from totalitarianism and our own souls from the materialistic desert in which they now wander" (*CC* 141). He calls for a "reconstruction of Christian theology" to forge "new symbols" for a "new vision of God" (*CC* 145, 148). Scientists must develop "a genuine synthesis of knowledge" and from it formulate new "concepts of God-as-purpose and God-as-origin." Like modern St. Pauls, they must reunite "rational humanism and uncritical faith," and make "a mystical approach to a vision of God" compatible with "modern scientific discoveries" and intelligible to a scientific, industrial society (*CC* 153-56). It is, perhaps, the refusal of science to undertake this commission that has led MacLennan to search for a theology of mediation, a redefinition of God for modern society, in the world of his fiction.

This summary of MacLennan's theology taken from his essays is intended to illustrate not only how intense his religious concerns were, but also how strongly his personal beliefs influenced the themes of his books and his didactic preoccupations determined the forms of his fiction. MacLennan's personal pilgrimage of faith from Calvinism to Christian existentialism is deeply embodied in the existential situation of his fictional characters; when he allows the drama of human struggle to carry his didactic theme, it can be very effective. Too often, however, his Protestant tendency to sermonize results in thesis-driven novels.

Before considering MacLennan's fiction as a product of his religious perspective, let us briefly examine the validity of that perspective. MacLennan's theory that the totality of the Canadian culture and character has been stifled by the repressive doctrines and puritanical psychology of

Calvinism is by no means original. But it is a simplistic generalization with which many Canadian theologians and church historians would not agree: "Religious pluralism is apparently as much a Canadian as an American phenomenon" (Grant 341). As D. J. Dooley has pointed out in *Moral Vision in the Canadian Novel*, critics from E. K. Brown to D. G. Jones and writers such as Margaret Laurence, Robertson Davies and Marian Engel have also made complaints against puritanism. But in this very complex socio-religious subject the questions must arise:

> [H]ow, when, and why did Canadian writers and critics come to take such a narrow view of this phenomenon as they actually do, and how did these writers and critics come to decide that puritanism coloured the moral outlook of all Canadians, from sea even to sea, no matter what their racial origins and religious backgrounds? (159)

MacLennan seems to have generalized from his particular experience as a Cape Breton Presbyterian to the national character in a sociological over-simplification, just as he habitually extended his detailed descriptions of Eastern Canada into a national panorama. Therefore his perspective has limited validity as Canadian socio-history, but as deeply felt personal experience it can be convincingly transmuted into fiction.

While the powerful, emotional denunciation of Calvinism in MacLennan's novels may not strike a responsive chord in all Canadians, his quest for a new theology in our post-Christian culture has universal significance. MacLennan's solution to the problem of writing a religious novel in a godless society was a redefinition of God to answer the modern questions about meaning and purpose within the existential situation of his characters. This emphasis on natural and liberal theology, as opposed to revealed and neo-orthodox theology, reveals an affinity with that branch of modern Protestantism most commonly identified with Paul Tillich and New Theology. Although there is no evidence in MacLennan's writings of any direct indebtedness to the theologian, Tillich's ideas strongly influenced liberal Protestant thought in North America from the 1940s to the present.

Tillich believed that communication of the Gospel today is possible only if one understands and participates in "the situation of existential conflict — the conflicts in the very depths of our human existence of longings, of anxiety, and of threatening despair" (*Theology* 207). Therefore all modern theology must be a "theology of mediation" between the religious tradition and the modern mind (*Perspectives* 209). In *The Courage to Be* Tillich says that, following the "death of God," twentieth-century man "has lost a meaningful world and a self which lives in meanings out of a spiritual centre." If he is creative "he reacts with the courage of despair, the courage to take his despair upon himself and to resist the radical threat of non-being by the courage to be as oneself" (138). This is Tillich's definition of modern existentialism. Another reaction to the threat of non-being, however, has been the rise of neo-collectivist systems: "Fascism, Nazism and Communism." The "courage to be as a part" gives to masses of people the courage to affirm themselves as participants in a collective that transcends death, gives meaning to life, and replaces for them "the God of judgment, repentance, punishment and forgiveness" (99-104).

However, according to Tillich (and MacLennan would agree), as faiths for the twentieth century, "the courage to be as a part" and "the courage to be as oneself" are ultimately disappointing: "the former, if carried through radically, leads to the loss of the self in collectivism and the latter to the loss of the world in Existentialism" (150-51). Therefore, Tillich offers an alternative. This is the "courage to be" which "is the courage to accept oneself as accepted in spite of being unacceptable," and which also takes into itself death and meaninglessness. The source of this courage is "absolute faith . . . which has been deprived by doubt of any concrete content." But this act of the courage to be is a manifestation of "the ground of being" which is God, and "the content of absolute faith is the God above God." This new vision of God transcends the old doctrines of theism: God as a vague symbol, God as a Person in the divine-human encounter, and "the God Nietzsche said had to be killed because nobody can tolerate being made into a mere object of absolute knowledge and absolute control" — MacLennan's Calvinist God. Rather, "the courage to be is rooted in the God who appears when God has disappeared in the anxiety of doubt" (160-83).

This brief outline of Tillich's thought, tracing the modern spiritual pilgrimage from theism to a reconstructed theology, a modern Christian existentialism, demonstrates the parallels between MacLennan's themes in his essays and fiction and these contemporaneous ideas in Protestant theology. The religious novelist's principal dilemma is realistically to portray the action of grace in nature. The positive result of this modern theological perspective for MacLennan's fiction is that he compassionately identifies with and explores the spiritual struggles of his characters within their existential reality. The negative aspect is that MacLennan's view of God, like that of New Theology, is both philosophically idealistic and personally subjective, and therefore difficult to dramatize. Tillich, for example, has repudiated "those elements in the Jewish-Christian tradition which emphasize the person-to-person relationship with God": the personalistic image of God, the personal nature of human faith and divine forgiveness, the idea of a divine purpose, and the person-to-person character of prayer and practical devotion (*Courage* 177).

These qualities, which have traditionally been portrayed by religious writers to dramatize God's interaction with this world (for example, in the works of the Catholic novelists, Greene and Mauriac), seem also to be absent from MacLennan's concept of God. His "practical Jesus" is an ethical model but not divine (*CC* 147), and God is discussed as a philosophical hypothesis

of human evolutionary intellect (D. Cameron, "MacLennan" 133), or a
subjective emotional experience most often stimulated by nature (*SR* 171-72).
In other words, in MacLennan's new theology, God is that synthesis of
science and mysticism which modern society can accept (*CC* 153-56), but He
is not a Person with an objective reality independent of human perception of
Him. A relationship with this transcendent, impersonal Deity is difficult to
portray dramatically. This is one of the reasons why, when MacLennan
portrays the existential questions with great realism, complexity, and
conviction, his theological resolutions often seem arbitrary and unconvincing.

MacLennan's greatest assets as a novelist are the traditional virtues of
interesting plots, well-realized characters, narrative action pieces, and vivid
settings that were his professed aim as a realistic writer:

> First, the satisfying novel must entertain them; it must so grip them that
> when they enter the book they cannot be easy until they have finished it.
> Then it must make the reader a part of the world of the novelist's creation,
> and this it does by creating fictional characters more real than the reader's
> personal friends. In order to make characters like these, the novelist must
> also create the backgrounds and locales in which the characters move, and
> make them consistent and vivid. (*SR* 146-47)

Unfortunately his greatest defect, and this often subverts his virtues, is that
MacLennan was first and foremost an essayist. As I noted in the Introduction,
he comes from a Protestant heritage that privileges the preaching of the Word
and the conversion of the audience. The tension between his didacticism and
his realism is constantly felt in his works. Although this dual commitment
results in technical weaknesses, it also gives his books the universal layers of
meaning that "if they do not make them great, at least make them much more
than ordinary romantic-idealist novels intended for well-meaning members of
the Book-of-the-Month Club" (Woodcock, *MacLennan* 51). However, the
tension between faith and fiction may partly account for the fact that
MacLennan's novel writing became increasingly slower and more laboured
over the years ("Story" 35-39).

The essential pattern that emerges from MacLennan's fiction is
remarkably similar to that which the *Literary History of Canada* describes as
characteristic of those "spiritual biographies" written in Canada between 1880
and 1920:

> The novel traces his [the central character's] doubts, loss of faith, and his
> search for a new religious position, unorthodox and undogmatic, or for
> some substitute "religion." The chief problems are the inspiration of the
> Bible, the presence of pain and evil in the universe, and the divinity of
> Christ; solutions are found in Pantheism, Universalism, and a belief in
> "Brotherhood," "true Christianity," the "living Jesus of the Gospels."
> (Roper, Schieder, Beharriell 306)

For in many ways MacLennan's "old-fashioned" novels are fighting the theological battles of the nineteenth century. His heroes repudiate the doctrines of Calvinism but cannot free themselves from its psychological legacy of guilt; they deny the reality of God in the world, and then desperately search for alternative "religions" to console their emptiness and anxiety. But all humanist solutions — social, political, materialistic, even personal relationships — ultimately fail them and they must eventually find a spiritual Absolute to give their lives meaning and purpose. This general pattern is developed in progressive stages — and growing disillusionment — through MacLennan's seven published novels.

2. *Barometer Rising*

After two amateurish and unpublished novels, "So All Their Praises" and "A Man Should Rejoice," MacLennan abandoned international settings to accept his wife's advice to write about his homeland. Recalling *Barometer Rising*, MacLennan explained what his philosophy as a rare Canadian novelist had to be in 1939:

> [I]t seemed to me that for some years to come the Canadian novelist would have to pay a great deal of attention to the background in which he set his stories. He must describe, and if necessary define, the social values which dominate the Canadian scene, and do so in such a way as to make them appear interesting and important to foreigners. Whether he liked it or not, he must for a time be something of a geographer, an historian and a sociologist, to weave a certain amount of geography, history and sociology into his novels. Unless he did this his stories would be set in a vacuum. He could not, as British and American writers do, take his background values for granted, for the simple reason that the reading public had no notion what they were. He must therefore do more than write dramas, he must also design and equip the stage on which they were to be played. (*TT* 52)

As Elspeth Cameron points out, the key phrase is "whether he liked it or not," but MacLennan "made a virtue of necessity" and became a "nationalist" author (*Life* 148). *Barometer Rising* (1941), therefore, is more than a wartime love story; it is an exemplum of Canada's maturation as a country during World War I and a prophecy of her future as the keystone in a great North Atlantic arch uniting the best of the old and new worlds, Britain and the United States. Unfortunately, the didactic content of the stage directions often threatens to destroy the drama of this thinly-veiled "national allegory" (Woodcock, *Introducing* 87).

The hero, Neil Macrae, represents a young Canada, betrayed by colonial powers in a destructive war, but returning home to establish his honour and independence as a leader in the new world order. Wounded, victimized, and humiliated by "the old men who were content to let it [Canada] continue second-rate indefinitely, looting its wealth while they talked about its infinite opportunities" (*BR* 323), Neil, in returning to Canada, is "identifying himself with the still-hidden forces which were doomed to shape humanity" in the future (*BR* 324). In a nationalistic outpouring, "modelled on John of Gaunt's patriotic speech from *Richard II* " (E. Cameron, *Life* 144), Neil celebrates post-colonial Canada:

> [T]his anomalous land, this sprawling waste of timber and rock and water where the only living sounds were the footfalls of animals or the fantastic laughter of a loon, this empty tract of primordial silences and winds and erosions and shifting colours, this bead-like string of crude towns and cities tied by nothing but railway tracks, this nation undiscovered by the rest of the world and unknown to itself, these people neither American nor English, nor even sure what they wanted to be, this unborn mightiness, this question-mark, this future for himself, and for God knew how many millions of mankind! (*BR* 120)

Militantly opposed to him is his uncle Geoffrey Wain, "the descendent of military colonists who had remained essentially a colonist himself, never really believing that anything above the second rate could exist in Canada, a man who had not thought it necessary to lick the boots of the English but had merely taken it for granted that they mattered and Canadians didn't" (*BR* 310). Significantly, the Wain family is also a leading representative of Canadian Calvinism. Respectable churchgoers, snobbish and materialistic, they are symbolized by their "ancestral establishment" which "patterned most of them and held them down" and represents "an incubus" to the heroine, Penny Wain (*BR* 29-30). She has been forced to hide her love for Neil and the fact of their illegitimate child under a puritanical cloak of hard work and self-denial. The "*massive* hypocrisy on the part of the Canadian Calvinists," especially in sexual matters, that has always angered MacLennan (D. Cameron, "MacLennan" 133) is typified in Colonel Wain's protection of Penny's reputation because she is "something belonging to him" (*BR* 98) while at the same time he is engaged in a sordid affair with his secretary.

As MacLennan has said, "the background is the most essential part" of *Barometer Rising* (*TT* 53), and in the melodramatic plot that resolves the conflicts between the old and young generations, Halifax is the chief protagonist. For centuries exploited by the British in wartime and ignored in peacetime, the colonial outpost "would do its duty by the English as long as there was an England left" (*BR* 74). It is the Halifax Explosion at 9:00 a.m. Thursday, December 6, 1917, that shatters all of the rigid structures of colonial society and destroys the power of Geoffrey Wain over the future of Neil and Penny. The explosion symbolizes the destructive, meaningless war into which Canada has been betrayed by her colonial mentality and the collusion of her churches and her "megalomaniac" "old men." However the war, like the explosion, is "catastrophic but not tragic" for Canada. She is "innocent" of the cause of the sociological suicide that is destroying Europe and of the "intolerable burden of guilt" which the Old World must bear. Canada will forge a new independence and even give Britain "a new birth" (*BR* 300).

Neil and Penny are the natural leaders of this future. He has roots in the honest, devout, archaic soil of Cape Breton (typified by the gentle giant, Alec MacKenzie). But they are also cosmopolitan: "two people who could seem at home almost anywhere, who had inherited as a matter of course and in their own country the urbane and technical heritage of both Europe and eastern United States" (*BR* 310). Scientifically educated (Neil at the Massachusetts Institute of Technology) and sexually liberated, now free from the hypocrisies of conventional religion, they confidently face the future, determined to preserve personal "integrity" and "dignity" and "to achieve a human significance in an age where the products of human ingenuity made mockery of the men who had created them" (*BR* 320-21).

While, as we have seen, this novel is primarily a secular story, there is an underlying theme that explores the purpose and meaning of life (a perennial concern for MacLennan), and that suggests a spiritual order behind our existential situation. The story is fraught with accidents and coincidences, of which the explosion is the catastrophic culmination. The hero is one of MacLennan's archetypal Odyssean "Wanderers" and Oedipal orphans, who has "long ago given up the attempt to discover a social or spiritual reason which might justify what had happened to himself and millions of others" during the War (*BR* 12). But MacLennan is not positing an absurdist universe. Neil still resists "the conviction that chance and preposterous accident had complete control of a man's life" and rejects Shakespeare's metaphor "that his life's continuance was as problematic as a fly's." Rather, it is "the final degradation of war that it could make a man's life appear so" (*BR* 201).

Similarly, Angus Murray, even drunk with a Halifax prostitute, clings to the hope suggested by his references to scripture and the old hymn "So, like the wanderer, the sun gone down, darkness be over me, my rest a stone," (*BR* 204) which, as Elspeth Cameron points out, has the optimistic ending "Yet in my dreams I'd be/Nearer, my God, to thee,/Nearer to thee" (*Life* 154). Disillusioned and demoralized by war, Murray nevertheless recognizes that "the beauty of the world remained and he found himself able to enjoy it" (*BR* 214), and he tries to reconcile the deaths around him "with a pattern possessing a wider meaning" (*BR* 309). Even the apparently capricious explosion reveals "a pattern" in Canadian society that has existed all along but required an "upheaval" to reveal its future direction:

> We're the ones who make Canada what she is today, Murray thought, neither one thing nor the other, neither a colony nor an independent nation, neither English nor American. And yet, clearly, the future is obvious, for England and America can't continue to live without each other much longer. Canada must therefore remain as she is, noncommittal, until the day she becomes the keystone to hold the world together. (*BR* 311)

In the end, the explosion has enabled both Angus and Neil to achieve personal dignity and independence. The Wanderer comes home, and his return is symbolically proclaimed as a new spiritual order, a "resurrection from the dead" (*BR* 205). But the spiritual theme in this novel remains a very muted backdrop to the national ideals. In 1941 MacLennan still believed that political forces could "shape humanity" and that Canada's barometer was rising so that "the day was inevitable" when the American heritage and the English heritage would unite in Canada and the country "would become the central arch which united the new order" (*BR* 325). Holding this humanist faith, he expects Neil and Penny to find personal salvation in political ideals and human love.

From this outline it should be obvious that MacLennan's preaching forces the characters and plot of this novel to carry a weight of didactic significance and commentary that sometimes cripples them. Much of the political optimism seems naive, elitist, and dated in retrospect, although his curious elimination of the French from this "half-American and half-English" Canada was partially remedied in his next novel. However, the real problem is that the main characters lack complexity and subtlety because they must function as thematic symbols and even then are beiaboured stereotypes:

> There was Geoffrey Wain, the descendant of military colonists. . . . There was Alec MacKenzie, the primitive man. . . . There were Penny and Neil Macrae, two people who could seem at home almost anywhere. . . . And there was himself, caught between the two extremes. . . . We're the ones who make Canada what she is today, Murray thought. . . . (*BR* 310-11)

Geoffrey Wain is too villainous, Penny too brilliant (yet not unfeminine since her prize-winning ship design is really Neil's), and Neil is too quickly transformed from shell-shocked victim to conquering hero to be quite believable. Criticism of MacLennan's coy treatment of sex is inevitable. But the love between Neil and Penny is not dramatically evoked either; it gets lost in the larger theme. In their final scene they are so engrossed in political sentiments that Penny does not even reveal that they have a daughter, while Neil is "identifying himself with the still-hidden forces" of Canadian nationalism (*BR* 324). Perhaps the child, also "still-hidden," symbolizes Canada's unknown future greatness (Woodcock, *Introducing* 98). Neil's final meditation is an example of the ventriloquism that the omniscient author performs throughout the novel, speaking long didactic passages through his characters in an undifferentiated voice and at times that are emotionally inappropriate. This defect in characterization seems to be a result of MacLennan's privileging of the Word as truth. For the minor figures who are untroubled by thematic speeches, for example, Uncle Alfred, Roddie, and especially Aunt Maria, are delightfully realistic. Aunt Maria's voice rings throughout the novel: "I ran into Mrs. Taylor this evening as we came out, that woman I was telling you about in the Red Cross. She's dreadful. People like that shouldn't be allowed to take part in the war" (*BR* 35).

The plot of *Barometer Rising* also suffers from thematic determinism. The characters' conflicts are never resolved dramatically in accordance with the logic of action or personality. Rather, after a series of contrived coincidences, the explosion operates as a *deus ex machina* to dispose of all the obstacles to Neil and Penny's happiness together. On the other hand, the plot is usually interesting, suspenseful, and full of documentary detail. The events leading up to the explosion are carefully structured and marked by dates and times, the movement of men and ships, so as to increase our suspense and foreshadow the cataclysm. The description of the actual explosion and subsequent rescue work is one of the most powerful action narratives in our literature. Indeed, the action and atmosphere of Halifax in 1917 are vividly conveyed throughout the book, and the city, as MacLennan wished, is the most fully realized character.

3. *Two Solitudes*

In *Two Solitudes* (1945) MacLennan continues the thematic pattern of a movement from Calvinism to a spiritual humanism in a denunciation of the old puritanical religions which he believes have sown the racial hatreds in this country, and in a quest for a meaningful faith for the individual in this scientific age. At the beginning of this novel, the country that was to have united the world is having serious problems with its own unity and the rift is largely religious: "You see the Methodists in Toronto and the Presbyterians in the best streets of Montreal and the Catholics all over Quebec, and nobody understands one damn thing except that he's better than everyone else" (*TS* 28). The conflict for the future of Quebec, and symbolically of Canada, is dramatically centred on the small parish of Saint-Marc-des-Érables. The opposing forces are puritanical Catholicism (Jansenism) and materialistic Calvinism, and the first protagonist is eventually trapped and tragically destroyed in the middle.

Father Beaubien, the parish priest, represents the paternalistic authority of the Church, jealously guarding the piety of an insular, pre-industrial, agrarian existence:

His mind moving slowly, cautiously as always, the priest visioned the whole of French-Canada as a seed-bed for God, a seminary of French parishes

speaking the plain old French of their Norman forefathers, continuing the
battle of the Counter-Reformation. . . . Let the rest of the world murder itself
through war, cheat itself in business, destroy its peace with new inventions
and the frantic American rush after money. Quebec remembered God and
her own soul, and these were all she needed. (*TS* 7-8)

Representing Anglo-American big business, an English war, and an alien
religion, Huntly McQueen is his natural adversary: "an Ontario Presbyterian
[a minister's son] he had been raised with the notion that French Canadians
were an inferior people, first because they were Roman Catholic, second
because they were French" (*TS* 14). He is a discreet member of the Montreal
financial elect, "Presbyterians to a man," who control the economy and
technology of modern industrial Canada from their offices on Saint James
Street and their massive stone houses on the slopes of Mount Royal (*TS* 92).

Athanase Tallard, the protagonist of the first half of this novel, is
caught between the forces of the past and the future. As a Member of
Parliament he has tried to bring Quebec into the mainstream of twentieth-
century North America, even supporting conscription and earning the enmity
of his fellow Québecois. Then, having failed politically to achieve unity, he
decides to ally himself with McQueen in using science "to crack the shell of
Quebec." In this he deliberately identifies himself "on the side of the future":
"Science was sucking prestige from the old age of faith and the soil. And
prestige was a matter of power." A factory in Saint-Marc-des-Érables would
raise its standard of living and give it social advantages under his enlightened
seigneurial direction:

> He knew what he wanted here: the factory would become the foundation of
> the parish, lifting the living standards, wiping out debts, keeping the people
> in their homes where they had been born, giving everyone a chance. It
> would enable them to have a model school that could provide modern
> scientific training. Then they would have a hospital, a public library, a
> playground, finally a theatre as the parish grew into a town. It would be a
> revolution, and he would be the one to plan and control it. (*TS* 88-89)

However, Athanase also has a scarcely admitted personal reason for
an alliance with the English which will bring him into direct conflict with
Father Beaubien: "his arguments for science were little more than arguments
against a religion he had rejected. And he had rejected it chiefly because of
his resentment against the power of the priests" (*TS* 69-70). Athanase has
adopted the ideas of the Enlightenment and the aphorisms of Voltaire and
Rousseau, replaced faith with reason and superstition with science (*TS* 74). He
had once dreamed of "bringing back something of the spirit of revolutionary
France to the older, wintry, clerical Norman France of Quebec" (*TS* 90). In
fact, Athanase is passionate, impetuous and arrogant; his temperament is

neither scientific nor rational. His basic motivation for rebellion against religion lies in his pride and desire for self-justification:

> His nature had always demanded a new idea of itself, and when he had his vigour, women had provided it. Now no woman could satisfy him, nor he a woman. Nothing was left him but principles and ideas. "God," he thought, "is that all there is to it? " And then it occurred to him that perhaps all wars and revolutions and movements of history started from sources just as trivial and undignified. He saw the people in their churches and nationalisms huddling together under flags and banners in desperate attempts to escape the knowledge of their own predicament. They were all silhouettes moving almost accidentally for seventy years or so over the ridge of the world between darkness and darkness. (TS 176-77)

For MacLennan, Athanase clearly represents the human condition searching for meaning and purpose to counteract the terrifying meaninglessness of man's existential plight. And, as a modern Québecois, he turns to "ideas" and even "nationalisms" rather than "churches" for his salvation.

MacLennan also supplies a secondary motive for Athanase's actions in his customary attack on puritanism. The English variety is denounced in a didactic interlude by Major Dennis Morey, who seems to exist in the novel solely to provide a token Western (Winnipeg) viewpoint on our puritan colonial mentality. Also, Calvinism is catalogued in the character of Janet Methuen, the villain of Part I, who is tragically inhibited, unnatural, unsexual, racist, self-righteous, and materialistic. But it is French-Canadian puritanism, Jansenism, against which Athanase rebels. As preached by Father Beaubien and sanctified by the late Marie-Adèle Tallard, it is a sexually repressive, life-denying doctrine that has perverted the natural instincts of both Marius and Athanase. However, Athanase refuses to accept the puritan judgement that condemns him for turning to Kathleen's life-giving love on the night his ascetic wife died. And, in part, that refusal leads to his rejection of the authority of his church: "No one should be frightened of God" (TS 150).

In his portrayal of the struggle between the simple piety of Father Beaubien and the modern intellectualism of Athanase Tallard, MacLennan paints the rural life of Saint-Marc-des-Érables as a hallowed pastoral existence, threatened by godless capitalism and technology, but in any case outmoded and doomed. Athanase's intellect has uprooted him from his religious and ancestral soil, and, like Canada after World War I, he wanders alien and alone into the twentieth century. In the end, betrayed and destroyed, his instincts lead him back home to his faith, his church and his people.

It is not as easy for his son Paul to come "home" in the second half of this novel. A child of two races, religions and legends, Paul, with Heather Methuen, obviously represents "the new Canada," the generation that came of age during the Depression (MacLennan's generation). And, in a repeated theme that characterizes MacLennan's novels, they must rebel against the repressions and stereotypes of their parents' prejudices which most often have been motivated or disguised by religion. Heather and Paul are both "the victims of the two racial legends within the country":

> It was as though the two sides of organized society had ganged up on them both to prevent them from becoming themselves. . . . On both sides, French and English, the older generation was trying to freeze the country and make it static. He supposed all older generations tried to do that, but it seemed worse here than any place else. Yet the country was changing. In spite of them all it was drawing together; but in a personal, individual way, and slowly, French and English getting to know each other as individuals in spite of the rival legends. (*TS* 270)

Paul's schizophrenic wanderings also represent Canada's search for identity and unity on the eve of World War II. He says (in another of MacLennan's invocations of the *Odyssey* myth):

> Science and war — and God knows what else — have uprooted us and the whole world is roaming. Its mind is roaming. . . . Its mind is going mad trying to find a new place to live. . . . I feel it — right here in myself. I've been living in the waiting room of a railway station. (*TS* 281)

In a world gone mad with Hitler, "the new city-hatred (contempt for all things but cleverness)," the impotence of the old leaders, and the worship of technology, Paul despairs of both the old theologies and "the new god" of politics:

> And behind Hitler, what? The machine. The magic worthy of every worship, mankind reborn for the service of efficiency, the still small voice of God the Father no longer audible through the stroke of the connecting rod, the suave omnipotent gesture of the hydraulic press, the planetary rumble of the conveyor belt, the visions of things to come — whole cities abolished in single nights, populations uplifted according to plan, cloudy blueprints of engineers, millions calling for help and millions for war, millions for peace and millions for suicide, and the grandeur and the efficiency and the solitude. (*TS* 306)

In the midst of such existential "loneliness" Paul and Heather must reject the "straightjackets" of their environment and forge their own identities, their "two solitudes" (*TS* 305), in order to realize the love defined in Rilke's epigraph to this novel, the love that will symbolically unite Canada while respecting its cultural differences:

> Love consists in this,
> that two solitudes protect,
> and touch, and greet each other.

Ironically, it is only by leaving the country that turns "religious denominations into flags" and weapons, and imposes a hypocritical puritan morality on the young, that Paul and Heather can find themselves and their own "personal religion" (*TS* 312). Then, destroying his first novel set amidst the disintegration of Europe, Paul brings his vision home to Canada. He rejects the modern gods of nationalism (represented by Marius) and materialism (typified by McQueen and Sir Rupert Irons) and commits himself to the unity of Canada, first in his writing and then by enlisting at the beginning of World War II. In this novel MacLennan still is optimistic that Canadian salvation, like personal salvation, can be achieved through self-knowledge, integrity, and humanist love.

Throughout *Two Solitudes* one wise old man, typically for MacLennan, has been the primary spokesman for the positive religious values in the novel, and through him the author again hints at a larger spiritual pattern which will eventually transcend humanist disillusionments. John Yardley is a committed Presbyterian who nevertheless strongly opposes the hypocrisies of puritanism with a healthy sexuality, an inclusive ecumenicism, a simple faith, and a personal integrity that earns the respect of both French and English. He has even, in the last years of his life, learned a non-puritan appreciation for beauty.

Yardley has recognized the existential loneliness that drives Athanase back to the faith of his fathers: "it means he got lonely and wanted to be what he'd been all his life, I guess. Or maybe it means something else so big I can't understand it" (*TS* 215). His term for this loneliness — the existential "fear" of "a mystery so darkly suggestive that no one can face it for long" — is "ultimate solitude." His metaphor for the spectre of potential meaninglessness and destructiveness of human life is his memory of the tropical sharks and barracudas "self-centred, beautiful, dangerous and completely aimless" (*TS* 61). Whereas Paul's solution for this "infinite waste of loneliness" is the human connection of "two solitudes" (*TS* 305), Yardley's dying meditation presents a theological answer to the "ultimate solitude." In the face of human evil and "ignorance," which is original sin ("on the whole the ordinary man was just as likely to choose the worst instead of the best"), humanist political solutions will not save the world: "Right at the end Jesus had given the plain warning not to expect too much of people" (*TS* 316). But acceptance of the "wonder" of life and of the "harmony of the whole" of life is necessary "to reconcile you to your own ignorance and to beautify the pattern in which you yourself were a part" (*TS* 317). This rejection of existential meaninglessness and subtle subversion of humanism in a celebration of God's creation and redemption foreshadow the ending of *The Watch That Ends the Night*.

Technically *Two Solitudes* is an example of the best and the worst of MacLennan's fiction as a product of his evangelistic didacticism. As Cockburn points out, the two halves of this novel are themselves solitudes (69). In Parts I and II the meaning generally arises out of the characters and the action; in Parts III and IV the theme dictates the characterization and the narrative. Athanase Tallard, one of the most successful of MacLennan's characterizations, dominates the first half of the novel. His conflicts with Father Beaubien and Huntly McQueen embody the theme within the dramatic action and dialogue and give the structure of this section a unity and tragic inevitability. There are very few obtrusively rhetorical passages of authorial comment. The minor characters are vividly realized. And the setting, which contrasts Saint-Marc-des-Érables and Montreal, is particularly effective in embodying the theme in concrete, visual correlatives of people and places.

However, having dramatically portrayed his concept of the French-Canadian problem, MacLennan felt compelled to orchestrate a solution. The main characters are romantic stereotypes (down to Paul's hair "foxed with grey" [*TS* 297]); Heather is an artist, Paul a novelist. They speak in the clichés of dimestore romances, and their relationship is contrived and static. Their development during the second half of the novel is the basis for its meaning, but they mature off-stage. The five years between Parts III and IV, crucial to our understanding of the characters, are only summarized in sketchy travelogues and the settings are just place names. There is practically no drama and no conflict in this section; even Paul's final confrontation with Janet is bloodless. Moreover, these "puppets" are "wired for sound" (Cockburn 45): their author's views on the main theme of Canadian unity, and several peripheral subjects such as the problems of Canadian novelists, the liberation of women, and the socio-economic reasons for World War II. Paul is modelled on MacLennan, and the hero's words are ironically appropriate for this half of the novel: "A novel should concern people, not ideas, and yet people had become trivial" (*TS* 307).

As most critics have noted, the two solitudes of this novel are a result of their dual protagonists (Athanase and Paul) and two different genres (national epic and *Künstlerroman*). But even the latter "portrait of the artist as a young man" is not allowed to develop organically because of MacLennan's national theme: "I wrote of a legend . . . this was not easy, and required endless re-writing, as the characters, once I had made my choice, had frequently to be rejected if their own lives interfered with the design I had felt at the beginning was true" (qtd. in E. Cameron, *Life* 188). Moreover, in these politically correct times, MacLennan's national theme has itself been criticized for its "ethnocentric bias" in stereotyping French Canadian nationalists and portraying as a symbolic ideal the unbalanced union of an English Canadian and an anglicized half-English Québecois. As Linda Leith concludes, not surprisingly, as a socio-political treatise "*Two Solitudes* is very much a product of its time" (32). Ultimately, the truth of MacLennan's novels lies not in political programmes but spiritual insights, a fact which he increasingly perceived and emphasized in subsequent novels as his faith in humanist solutions decreased.

4. *The Precipice*

The Precipice (1948) is really a religious thesis in the guise of the "sociological novel" that MacLennan felt was fashionable and marketable at the time (E. Cameron, *Life* 210). It is an analysis of the respective legacies of puritanism without God in Canada and the United States. The novel was written during the same period as his essay "How We Differ from Americans" (later reprinted as "On Discovering Who We Are") and illustrates the same didactic motive: "Many differences between Canadians and Americans it will do us good to recognize," and the same maxim: "Americans are proud of what they do. The excessive puritanism of Canadians makes them proud of what they don't do." He admits that the "puritanism which is still dominant in Canada has grown so weak in most parts of the United States, particularly in cities of the East and in California, that you could almost think the coat had been turned inside out" (*CC* 52-54). However, MacLennan intends to illustrate in this novel what he states in the Preface, that American materialistic achievements and sexual licence are also the inevitable result of "the journey which the puritans began more than three hundred years ago when they lost hope in themselves and decided to bet their lives on the things they could do rather than on the men they were" (viii). The novel is neatly divided into reciprocal halves. In Book I a visiting American liberates the Canadian heroine from her repressive Calvinist environment; in Books II, III and IV she attempts to free him from the tyranny of the puritan-inspired American Way of Life.

Book I is set in the summer of 1938 in Grenville, Ontario:

> Here was lodged the hard core of Canadian matter-of-factness on which men
> of imagination had been breaking themselves for years. Grenville was sound,
> it was dull, it was loyal, it was competent — and, oh, God, it was so Canadian!
> . . . Until the Grenvilles of Canada were debunked from top to bottom . . . there
> would be no fun and no future for anyone in the country. (*P* 8)

Here all the attributes of small-town "chocolate-brown" Calvinism — fear of emotions, reverence for proper appearances, and repressed sexuality — are invested in the house and family of John Knox Cameron. The "calvinistic horror" of his own childhood, the shame and guilt he had been taught, made him a lonely, frustrated, fearful man of "iron self-control" and rigid respectability. Although he has been dead seven years, his spirit still haunts the house which was his "symbol" and his "fortress," and bequeaths the "weight of the merciless religion" which his aunts had taught him to "the third generation," his daughters (*P* 50-53).

Jane Cameron has inherited her father's mantle as the "collective conscience" of the community: "it was one of Jane's talents to create at will an atmosphere in which everyone around her felt guilty" (*P* 103). She follows, "in thought and in life, all the principles of the religion and morality

which the entire Protestant part of the country professed to honor," but
compromised with privately. Since she has no experience of "great crimes,"
she has concentrated all her righteousness against sex, which she believes is
"the dirtiest thing in the world, and near to the root of all evil" (*P* 122). It is
only in her music that her "sublimated sexuality" finds an unconscious voice
(*P* 119).

However, Lucy Cameron, the heroine of this story, is determined to
"undo the chain of evil" which is their paternal legacy and to exorcise the past
from the present with the liberating power of "knowledge" and "love" (*P* 53).
She, in a foreshadowing of Catherine Carey (Mathews, "Ideology" 77), has
"learned the beginning of understanding" and a celebration of life during her
years of teenage illness (*P* 52). She has painted the Cameron house blue and
white, and found joy in the beauty of nature and her gardens — a kind of
prelapsarian beauty "which exists almost without knowledge of good and evil,
probably the only kind possible in a puritan town" (*P* 54). But her love for the
vigorous, young American, Stephen Lassiter, brings her to a confrontation
between her desire for freedom and self-fulfilment, and the full weight of
hypocritical Calvinist shame and respectability. When Jane demands that she
keep up "appearances" so that people might respect them, Lucy answers:
"Respect us? For what we do? Or for what we don't do?" (*P* 148). However,
Lucy is "unable to discard the superstitious sense of taboo under which she had
been reared" in order to marry the divorced Stephen (*P* 156). At this point she
turns for advice to Matt McCunn, her father's antithesis, who is a defrocked
Presbyterian minister. His condemnation of Calvinist hypocrisy, and his
encouragement of her surrender to her "perfectly natural" desires (*P* 162) enable
her to accept the new life with Stephen.

MacLennan's indictment of Calvinism, offered through Lucy and
McCunn, mainly rests on its perversion of the response to the first proposition
of the Catechism — "*Man's chief end is to glorify God and enjoy Him
forever!*" This "great and noble" other side of the Presbyterian faith celebrates
the joy of doing "the will of God" (*P* 143). However, as McCunn points out,
"the information they got on that subject all came from John Calvin, and all
he told them was what not to do" (*P* 161). In this atmosphere of frustration,
failure and guilt, the law of morality takes precedence over the spirit of love.
Nevertheless, in a prophecy that MacLennan felt was later fulfilled (*CC* xi),
he warns Canada:

> God help a people if they think sex is the only important sin there is, for the
> day will come when they find they've been lied to and cheated, and then
> they'll cut loose and make a mockery of sex and go straight to hell the way
> the Romans did. Don't forget . . . the old Romans were puritans too! (*P* 163)

As Lucy discovers when she follows Stephen to the United States, this
is precisely what has happened in the American cities; their legacy from

Calvin is equally destructive. Breaking away from traditional religion, they worship the new gods of technology, materialism, and sex. Religion which has stopped "paying off" is scrapped (*P* 115), and God has become "irrelevant" in the concrete cathedrals of New York (*P* 181).

Carl Bratian — seducer, exploiter and destroyer — is the high priest of this new religion (and another antithesis of Matt McCunn), the quintessential American adman:

> He claimed that America was developing into a modern Roman Empire. . . .
> "The bigger the country gets, the less sure of himself every individual in it is going to become. All right. Go hard for nationalism. Go hard for sex. Go hard for efficiency. . . . But don't forget this — the only thing *all* of them are interested in is sex." (*P* 244)

Bratian's rags-to-riches story is the American Dream, but MacLennan reveals its hollow core: "nobody except himself seemed to know in his bones that life was completely without meaning" (*P* 247). Only Lucy recognizes the villain of this novel as she warns Stephen "there's death in a man like Carl. Ultimately he kills whatever he touches. And the worst thing about him is that he knows exactly what he's doing" (*P* 275).

The second half of the novel takes place in the United States during and after World War II. In this "season of the universal payoff" the "well-meaning generation" is confronted with its own terrible inadequacy and mortality. Speaking through Stephen's sister Marcia, MacLennan makes the same point as in several of his essays: "We thought science had arrived to take the place of religion, and we believed the only thing needed to make us good was a good economic system" (*P* 217). The ultimate result of such beliefs is portrayed in the desperate, meaningless lives of Marcia, Carl Bratian, and Stephen Lassiter. And the new gods of money and sex eventually destroy Lucy's marriage.

Stephen Lassiter is the new technological man. His "factual engineer's mind" comprehends the skills and values of "this world the engineers had made" and also shares the "tensions" produced by their accomplishments (*P* 348-49). For the results of this materialist, technological drive are symbolized in the horror of the atomic bomb and "the destruction of Hiroshima"; in Jane's words, "the Americans were bound to do something like that one day" (*P* 347).

Stephen has liberated Lucy from the repressions of Canadian Calvinism, but he is still bound to the puritanical legacy inherited from his father and celebrated as the American way of life:

> In America there were no limits, or none that Stephen had ever recognized. Apparently he had always expected something new around every corner and had been reared to consider himself a failure unless he found it: more money

to make, more ideas to try out, more women to sleep with, more rules to smash, more impossibilities to make commonplace.(*P* 301)

MacLennan captures this relentless American progress in the title metaphor which he has already connected with "the Gadarene swine" — "the most progressive animals the world had ever seen" (*P* 16). Lucy articulates this theme:

> The other night after we heard about the atomic bomb I began to think of the Americans . . . like a great mass of people and not as individuals. I saw them moving in a vast swarm over a plain. They had gone faster and farther than any people had ever gone before. Each day for years they had measured out the distance they'd advanced. They were trained to believe there was nothing any of them had to do but keep on travelling in the same way. And then suddenly they were brought up short at the edge of a precipice which hadn't been marked on the map. There they were with all their vehicles and equipment, jostling and piling up on the front rank. . . . And there was Stephen himself, heaving and pushing without realizing the significance of what he was doing, in a rank not very far from the front. (*P* 360-61)

Her vision echoes a MacLennan essay also published in 1948:

> America's crisis, and therefore the crisis of the rest of us, consists in this: puritanism has conditioned its members to act rather than to think, to deal with means rather than with ends, to press forward with ever-increasing speed and efficiency toward a material goal. Today, after having advanced further into a materialistic paradise than any other people, Americans find themselves staring over the edge of a precipice, unable to make up their minds where to go. (*CC* 81-82)

Despite the sociological veneer, *The Precipice* ultimately portrays the failures of modern society — meaningless materialism, purposeless technological progress, and sterile sex — as a religious problem. Marcia's long didactic analysis of her religious conversion is MacLennan's obituary for his own "well-meaning generation" (*P* 305-9):

> For three hundred years we've lived on this continent in that same puritan tradition without ever knowing ourselves forgiven, and that's why we've become so callous and hard and rebellious. Even when we no longer believe in the God of our ancestors, the old guilt-habit stays. That's the trouble with Steve and I know it's the trouble with me — trying to run away from ourselves, not by finding something better but just trying to escape. (*P* 305)

However, escapism into the "unspent pleasures" of sex, or the absolution of a "materialist" psychoanalyst brings neither forgiveness nor salvation to their lives. Marcia's revelation is that:

> No *man* may deliver another from evil — only God can do it. And all of us keep right on killing ourselves by the sin of pride, all of us claiming we have

a monopoly on deliverance — communists, socialists, democrats — all of us
playing at being God. (*P* 307)

It is because "proud" Protestantism has failed to provide absolution for, and
an alternative to, the failures of humanism, that Marcia has "renounced all that
her forebears had stood for by going back to incense and authority and the
high altar, led by an Irish priest from the streets of New York" (*P* 308).

The religious rhetoric is awkwardly integrated into the fiction. But
the theological theory is actually quite complex and sophisticated. As Paul
Tillich explains it, the "autonomy" of reason, which during the
Enlightenment came to oppose the "heteronomy" (foreign or external
authority) of the Catholic Church, still retained the dimension of
"theonomy" (our personal experience of the divine Spirit) in Protestantism,
even in Calvinism. "Autonomy which is aware of its divine ground is
theonomy, but autonomy without the theonomous dimension degenerates
into mere humanism." The breaking up of ecclesiastical heteronomy and
the loss of theonomy (MacLennan's "God of our ancestors") have led to an
"empty autonomy" (the humanism of the "well-meaning generation"), and
the "danger of grasping securities given by false authorities and totalitarian
powers" (*Perspectives* 24-28). This is the same warning that MacLennan
gives against false modern gods, political and economic.

The implication in the novel, however, is that, while Marcia has found
happiness in her conversion, a return to the authorities of ecclesiastical
heteronomy is not the way to theonomy for most of MacLennan's
contemporaries. And with this analysis of modern capitalistic society Tillich
is in complete agreement:

Theonomy, originally signifying a law or validity with divine sanction in
contrast to the law emanating from the self or autonomy, has in
contemporary discussion acquired a more definite meaning. It is sharply
distinguished from heteronomy, i.e., from the shattering of autonomously
validated forms of human thought and action by a law alien and external to
the spirit. Theonomy is in contrast to heteronomy an imbuing of
autonomous forms with transcendent import. It originates not through the
renunciation of autonomy, as does, for example, the Roman Catholic idea of
authority, but only through the deepening of autonomy in itself to the point
where it transcends itself. The transcending of the autonomous forms in
culture and society, their being impressed or imbued by a principle
supporting and at the same time breaking through them but not shattering
them: that is theonomy. . . . The struggle for the idea of tolerance on the soil
of capitalistic society destroys the political power of heteronomy and gives
to the autonomous principles a possibility of free development. But
autonomy left to its own devices leads to increasing emptiness and — since
there cannot be a vacuum even in the spiritual realm — it finally becomes
imbued with demonically destructive forces. The insight into this whole

complex of cultural development has led to the demand for a new theonomy. (trans. and qtd. in Adams 60-61)

In America's "capitalistic society" Stephen's "autonomy" and the resultant spiritual "vacuum" have led to his "demonically destructive forces" of ambition and sex to take the place of religion. Now, betrayed by his material gods ("it wasn't as if he hadn't worked hard all his life" [*P* 352]), disillusioned with his value system ("wanting to be liked, wanting to be admired for doing a good job was so much too little in this world" [*P* 355]), left "dangling between" the guilt of the past and the failure of the present (*P* 354), Stephen gropes for some kind of personal integrity. He has reached the same depths of self-disgust that Marcia experienced before her miracle: "You know, you have to be very wrong, you have to wound yourself and be completely lost and abandoned and then forgiven before you can see God" (*P* 309).

At the end of the novel Lucy represents "what the church means when it talks of Grace" (*P* 309) when she offers Stephen and his generation a symbolic absolution for their sins. In a didactic finale Lucy returns to Stephen and reviews all of the themes of this novel. She includes Stephen and Jane in a general condemnation of the evils of puritanism ("the same refusal to believe that Christ had meant what he said when he stated that the kingdom of heaven belonged to the poor in spirit") and its antithesis, the rebellion into empty autonomy. Stephen would continue the cycle with more misery, "taking upon himself a devious, useless punishment for a useless, ancient guilt" (*P* 371). However, Lucy's forgiveness and acceptance of him demonstrate that not by works but "by grace are ye saved through faith, not of yourselves; it is a gift of God" (*P* 370). Stephen's response to the offer of "grace" — that is, his "faith" — is extremely ambiguous. It is by no means clear that he has arrived at Lucy's spiritual freedom, the new theonomy which is Tillich's "courage to be": "the courage to accept oneself as accepted in spite of being unacceptable" (*Courage* 160). But Lucy is encouraged enough to offer a benediction: "it's a beginning" (*P* 372).

If this theological analysis of this novel is valid, it should be obvious that, while MacLennan presents a sophisticated and comprehensive theology, the plot and characters suffer from the tyranny of the Word. *The Precipice* is a transitional novel for MacLennan in which the personal religious vision, which we have identified in Angus Murray and Captain Yardley as a subtext in their novels, is foregrounded as the solution to the failures of politics and humanism. Unfortunately, despite his reliance on rhetoric, MacLennan never clearly defines either the problem or the solution in dramatic terms. The plot is too obviously structured and schematic. The first part is more interesting because there is more action, but it is a conventional Cinderella romance, complete with two jealous sisters and trite dialogue and situations. The second half exists too often as an excuse for MacLennan's sermonizing, so that "the American chapters of *The Precipice* remind one of a Victorian cautionary novel" (Woodcock, *MacLennan* 88).

The point of view is also problematic. Book II changes the narrative centre from Lucy and Stephen to Bruce Fraser, and Book III surveys the war years through six different consciousnesses. Consequently, when we return to Stephen and Lucy, we have only the author's analysis of their marriage breakdown and little sense of the dramatic development during their crucial seven years together. We are never convinced, therefore, by the theme that MacLennan is so obviously manipulating them toward: "Lucy began to wonder if one of the causes of her failure to hold Stephen's love might not simply be the fact that he was an American and she was not" (*P* 301).

The characters in the novel tend to operate as authorial spokespersons and allegorical symbols. Bruce Fraser, another of MacLennan's writer-philosopher alter egos (previewing George Stewart), always remains peripheral to the plot. Parallel to Lucy, contrasting with Stephen, he exists primarily to inject MacLennan's socio-political set-pieces (echoes of his essay) into the novel: analyses of war (*P* 227), Europe (*P* 344), modern literature (*P* 332-33), and especially Canada (*P* 8, 225, 345). By the end of the novel, Marcia's conversion and the reunion between Lucy as personified grace and Stephen as unregenerate nature seem more theologically predestined than dramatically inevitable.

While provocative, MacLennan's theme is too ambitious in its generalizations from particulars. His analysis of small-town Canadian puritanism is accurate and realistic; his portrait of sleepy Grenville, with the cameos of Jane Cameron and her antithesis Matt McCunn, is the best thing in the novel. But his implied reduction of the complex subject of Canadian-American relations to the marriage of one decent, small-town, Ontario, Presbyterian spinster and one corrupt, big-city, New England, atheistic adman falsifies the intricacies of the issues. Robin Mathews insists:

> MacLennan doesn't choose to deal with terms he sets up for himself: U.S. economic imperialism, an inhumane technology displacing working people, and the meaning to innocent populations and individuals of the mad, murdering armies of the Second World War during which the novel is set. The monstrous evil done to those populations and individuals is briefly explained by "their refusal to solve their individual problems." ("Ideology" 82)

This sociological reductionism is a result of MacLennan's theological idealism and subjectivism. His characters repeatedly ascribe all of American's "progress," including the atomic bomb, to its puritan heritage. But, as MacLennan himself has pointed out, there are many other historical factors involved:

Americans are more optimistic, both about themselves and about their country, than Canadians are. The reason for this may be partly climatic, but most of it is historical. The United States was formed as the result of a successful revolution. Since that time it has never lost a war. Most of its great projects have been successful. (*CC* 53)

5. *Each Man's Son*

Each Man's Son (1951) recapitulates most of the author's previous criticisms of Calvinism, both as a theology and as a crippling psychological complex, and he again probes the existential meaninglessness that accompanies a renunciation of religion. This time he offers a solution, based not on abstract dogma nor religious rhetoric, but on the dramatically satisfying resolution of human relationships.

For the most part, MacLennan has confined his authorial didacticism in this novel to the Prologue. (According to his biographer, he was relieved that he need no longer be "a geographer, an historian and a sociologist" and could turn to "universal" themes, but his publishers required him to provide a preface explaining Cape Breton and Calvinism, and he reluctantly agreed to this "introductory stuff" [E. Cameron, *Life* 230-31]). In it he introduces the beautiful but blighted world of Cape Breton Island, and the curse that dwells within the noble, exiled Highlanders:

> [A]n ancient curse, intensified by John Calvin and branded upon their souls by John Knox and his successors — the belief that man has inherited from Adam a nature so sinful there is no hope for him and that, furthermore, he lives and dies under the wrath of an arbitrary God who will forgive only a handful of His elect on the Day of Judgement. (*EM* x)

MacLennan goes on to analyze his protagonist before the fact. The Highlanders' response to this "curse upon their souls" is escape into "drink," "knowledge," or exile. Dr. Daniel Ainsley (who has chosen the second option at the beginning of the novel and the third by the end) is "a freethinker . . . proud because he had neither run away nor sought a new belief in himself through hard liquor." He has attempted to escape the "sense of sin, a legacy of the ancient curse . . . by denying God's existence." But "when he displayed his knowledge and intelligence as a priest displays his beads, he felt guilty because he knew so little and was not intelligent enough" (*EM* x-xi). In Tillich's terms, his works and empty autonomy cannot free him from existential guilt or yield the divine justification he seeks. So "each man's son" is driven by "the daemon which has made him what he is and the other daemon which gives him hope of becoming more than any man can ever be" (*EM* xi). In the theological pattern of this book the hero is trapped between the guilt of the past, the vengeful Father Jehovah, and the impossible ambition of the future, self-justification and salvation. Only through self-sacrificing love, identified with Christ and, as in *The Precipice*, symbolized by mother-figures, can the tragic trap be broken and Ainslie redeemed.

In his Cape Breton setting MacLennan vividly portrays this legacy of "Scotch Presbyterianism": in the superstitions of Jimmie MacGillivray who believes his stomachache is a "punishment for sin" (*EM* 41); and the intolerance of Mollie MacNeil's father who was an elder of the church but never spoke to her after her shotgun marriage (*EM* 34); and the hypocrisy of the miners who dutifully attend church after drinking and brawling the night before (*EM* 80). It is clear that their religion offers no consolation for the "blasphemy" of "fighting clans going into the blackness of the earth to dig coal" (*EM* 67), because it is based on a theology of fear. It denies "the promises of the New Testament" in deference to the Old: "For if God was love, what was to be done about Jehovah?" (*EM* 41). MacLennan's picture of the archetypal Calvinist, Mrs. MacCuish (*EM* 152-53), burns with "indignation at self-righteous puritans who would make little children feel guilty for their human nature, while at the same time withholding from them the release of confession and absolution" (*CC* 139).

Daniel Ainslie, despite his education (a symbolic escape from the evil of the mines) and his brilliance as a surgeon, has returned to Cape Breton and is, therefore, symbolically bound by the Calvinist paradox taught him by his father:

> The old Calvinist had preached that life was a constant struggle against evil, and his son had believed him. At the same time he had preached that failure was a sin. . . . How could a successful man be sinless, or a sinless man successful? (*EM* 85)

Ainslie resents his wife Margaret "because she hasn't been able to wash away" his sense of sin (*EM* 63). Therefore, he attempts to achieve redemption himself through medical skills and an exhausting workload. As another of MacLennan's wise old men tells him, "although he might be an intellectual agnostic, he was an emotional child in thrall to his barbarous Presbyterian past" (*EM* 64).

Dr. Dougald MacKenzie (the archetypal doctor-father of MacLennan's own life and the fictional heir to Captain Yardley, Angus Murray, and Matt McCunn) has overcome guilt with grace and reconciled science and religion, insisting "it was entirely possible for a scientific medical man of experience to believe in the efficacy of prayer" (*EM* 186). Another spokesman for MacLennan, he denounces Calvin's theology:

> Man, having through Adam's fall lost communion with God, abideth evermore under His wrath and curse except such as he hath, out of His infinite loving-kindness and tender mercy, elected to eternal life through Jesus Christ — I'm a Christian, Dan, but Calvin wasn't one and neither was your father. It may sound ridiculous to say, in cold words, that you feel

guilty merely because you are alive, but that's what you were taught to believe until you grew up. (*EM* 63)

But, in rejecting God's judgement, MacKenzie articulates the hope of the novel in Christ's mercy: "The old Celts knew as well as Christ did that only the sinner can become the saint because only the sinner can understand the need and the allness of love" (*EM* 66).

Ainslie, however, cannot believe in the love of a God whom he visualizes as cruel and predatory, "a tight-skinned dog with green eyes, standing before him with muscles rippling under its tawny hide" (*EM* 186). He decides to break "the circle of Original Sin" himself (*EM* 64), to assuage his guilt and worthlessness, the barrenness of his life and the purposelessness of his universe, with a son. Alan MacNeil will be his personal hope for past justification and future immortality, "the boy he himself might have been, the future he can no longer attain" (*EM* 83). Alan represents the son who is loved, forgiven, free of the ancient curse and without the knowledge of sin (*EM* 153). However, in an ironic repetition of the sins of his father, Ainslie is prepared to use Alan, and ruthlessly to deny the rights and the worth of his mother Mollie, in order to fulfil his ambitions. As Dr. MacKenzie warns him: "You aren't looking for a son, Dan. You're looking for a God" (*EM* 189).

As the plot unfolds, the "circle of Original Sin" eventually embraces everyone, as salvation through works proves fruitless, and sin and guilt lead to more sin without forgiveness and redemption to break the chain. MacLennan, in a typical (but in this novel infrequent) authorial interruption, comments on the action:

> If God looked down on them that summer, the kind of God their ministers had told them about, He must have been well pleased, for by summer's end all of them except Alan were conscious of their sins. Longing to do their best, they had discovered there is no best in this world. Yearning for love, they had found loneliness. Eager to help one another, they had made each other wretched. Dreaming of better lives, they had become totally discontented with the lives they led. (*EM* 200)

For Ainslie, sexual repression has corrupted his love for Margaret, and driving ambition has prevented their having children until it is too late, so that he has symbolically as well as physically sterilized his wife. Now, in trying to acquire a son, he arrogantly neglects the maternal rights of both Margaret and Mollie: "Mollie MacNeil is a good woman, but she'll never be more than what she is now, and Alan deserves far better than that. I'm the only one who can help him and nothing is going to stop me" (*EM* 190). For his wife, the "guilt of failure which every childless woman knows" is compounded by resentment at her husband's "growing fondness for another woman's son" (*EM* 201). Therefore, they are both driven to "the essence of sin" — "a wilful and inextricable involvement of the self in the lives of others" (*EM* 206).

Ainslie counsels Mollie to forget Archie MacNeil and then tries to usurp the affections of her son; Margaret advises her to save Alan from Ainslie by going off with Louis Camire. The tragic climax of this story occurs when the subplot concerning Alan's real father collides violently with the main plot around his surrogate father, and the deaths of three victims can be seen as an inevitable result of the selfish ambition of the protagonist.

Before the finale, however, Ainslie repents his actions and confronts the loss of Alan and the death of his hopes. He descends into a spiritual hell, furiously repudiating the Calvinist God and the "mad theologians" whose doctrines had "hobbled his spirit" and led him to "a fear of love" with their "ancient curse" (*EM* 219). But now he must face the existential anxiety of meaninglessness:

> If there was no God, then there was nothing. If there was no love, then existence was an emptiness enclosed within nothing. . . . [He contemplated] a world where there were no gods, no devils, no laws, no certainties, no beginnings and no end. A world without purpose, without meaning, without intelligence; dependent upon nothing, out of nothing, within nothing; moving into an eternity which itself was nothing. (EM 220)

Ainslie's reaction is a freedom of "the spirit": "It had been caught in a prison and now it was free. But its freedom was the freedom of not caring" (*EM* 220). In terms of Paul Tillich's theology, he has realized that " 'God is dead,' and with him the whole system of values and meanings in which one lived. This is felt as both a loss and as a liberation. It drives one either to Nihilism or to the courage which takes non-being into itself" (*Courage* 140). Ainslie experiences both:

> With longing for continuance brimming in his blood, he had looked ahead on his days and seen total emptiness. He had reached his core. And there he had stopped. He got to his feet and looked down at the brook. In that moment, he had made the discovery that he was ready to go on with life. (*EM* 220)

This decision Tillich calls "the courage to be as oneself" in its "most radical form" — modern existentialism (*Courage* 123): "the courage of despair, the experience of meaninglessness, and the self-affirmation in spite of them" (*Courage* 140). It is difficult to see how the critics can interpret Ainslie's "short paragraph" (quoted above) as "the rediscovery of faith" or "Christian humanism" (Dooley, "Daemon" 73). For it is clear that, with a new acceptance of his wife, his work, and his world that lacks the "continuance and permanency" of an earlier era, Ainslie places his confidence in science rather than religion: "He was now alone with his own skill, surer of his fingers than of his soul. . . . So he would go to Europe . . . and there he would reach the top of his profession" (*EM* 221).

However, after the violent climax of the novel in which Mollie is murdered, Ainslie realizes that his separate peace with life has still not freed him from the consequences of sin and guilt: "I killed her as surely as my father killed my mother. . . . Through arrogance, the both of us. Through total incapacity to understand that in comparison with a loving human being, everything else is worthless" (*EM* 243). Ainslie finally understands that "the circle of Original Sin" which caused this tragedy is the reality of human selfishness which Calvinism has simply magnified into a terminus. Sin can be forgiven and redeemed for "each man's son," however, in the "need and allness of love" (*EM* 66), the self-sacrificing love of Christ demonstrated by the three mother figures in the novel. Ainslie's final repentance and confession — "I love the boy" — now receive MacKenzie's blessing: "Yes, Dan. Now I think you do" (*EM* 244).

MacLennan has called *Each Man's Son* a "transitional piece" ("Story" 34), and in it we see the improvement in his craftsmanship between his worst novel and his best. I think this change occurs largely because MacLennan has convincingly embodied his religious theme in the existential struggle of a central protagonist and the consequent drama of human conflict. The main characters (except Camire) are no longer symbolic puppets with generalized national characteristics, but rounded individuals whose actions can be seen as consistent and believable. The multiple narrative centres have a unified focus, and give complexity and depth to MacLennan's analysis of the motivations of the characters. While his habitual theme of the puritan curse is emphasized in Ainslie, he does not restrict the psychology of any of his characters purely to that motivation. There are the inevitable didactic passages, most of which I have quoted. But these are few and short (compared to those in *The Precipice*), and generally integrated into the dialogue and reflected in the action. Ainslie's internal revelation, although sometimes belaboured, is convincing from an introspective, slightly neurotic intellectual. Aside from the author's interlude at the beginning of Chapter xxiii, the only false passage in the novel concerns Ainslie's existential philosophizing (*EM* 219-20) which is too abstract and ambiguous in its relation to the subsequent action (a preview of the problem in Part VII, Ch. iv of *The Watch That Ends the Night*).

There is certainly justification for MacLennan's Calvinist preoccupations in this novel set among the Scottish Presbyterians of this small Cape Breton community. Even then, except in the Prologue, he resists blanket generalizations and admits other factors in their psychology, most particularly hatred of the mines which become a satisfying symbolic correlative for the evil "corruption" of mankind (*EM* 67). The setting, the minor characters, and the local customs and dialect are reproduced with a detailed realism that demonstrates MacLennan's intimacy with his birthplace. And the character of Ainslie, no doubt, owes much to MacLennan's father, who was for many years a doctor in a Cape Breton mining town, an amateur Greek scholar, and "full of Scotch and Calvinist quirks" (*SR* 64).

The weakest part of the novel is the ending — melodramatic, violent, and too contrived in its convenient removal of Alan's parents. However, the tight structure (confined to the summer of 1913), alternating the main plot and sub-plot around the struggle for Alan, builds suspense. And the detailed characterization provides an artistic, if not emotional, inevitability for the plot resolution. In this novel, MacLennan achieved his best integration of religious vision and realistic form up to this point.

6. *The Watch That Ends the Night*

The Watch That Ends the Night (1959), MacLennan's finest novel, incorporates the whole thematic pattern which we have traced through his other fiction to the spiritual resolution which has been suggested in his essays: a radical redefinition of God to answer the existential dilemma of modern man. This novel represents MacLennan's theology for a post-Christian culture, and his solution for the realistic novelist's problem of writing a religious novel for a secular society. In it he retraces the spiritual autobiography which he feels was typical of his "well-meaning generation": the loss of faith and rebellion against the God of their ancestors, the resultant guilt and anxiety, the search for surrogate gods in politics, economics, personal integrity, and human love — all of which we have seen displayed in his previous novels as possible solutions to the human dilemma. But now he affirms the complete inadequacy of good works and humanist ideals as the ultimate salvation for existential emptiness. At the end of the novel, in the face of temporal pessimism, he proffers a vision of eternal transcendence which is foreshadowed in the title, taken from the old Protestant hymn based on Psalm 90:

> A thousand ages in thy sight
> Are like an evening gone.
> Short as the watch that ends the night
> Before the rising sun.
>
> O God, our help in ages past,
> Our hope for years to come;
> Be thou our guard while troubles last,
> And our eternal home!

MacLennan said that during the writing of this novel he shed "the intellectual skin" that his generation had worn:

> So long as I wore it myself, my novels had been essentially optimistic. I had believed the barometer was really rising; I had believed . . . that the two solitudes were bound to come together in Canada. But my last two novels

> [*The Watch That Ends the Night* and *Return of the Sphinx*] have been tragic.
> My original title for *The Watch* was a dead give-away: it was *Requiem*.
> Requiem for one I had loved who had died, but also for more: requiem for
> the idealists of the Thirties who had meant so well, tried so hard and gone so
> wrong. Requiem also for their courage and a lament for their failure on a
> world-wide scale. . . . What *The Watch* was trying to say in the atmosphere
> of its story was that the decade of the 1950's was the visible proof of my
> generation's moral and intellectual bankruptcy. ("Reflections" 31)

However, in the conclusion of the novel, his "intuitions" were also "asserting
that God had not been outmoded by the Christian Church, Bertrand Russell,
the social scientists and modern education" ("Reflections" 32). It is this hope
that he tried painstakingly to express in terms of realistic fiction.

In the face of the traumatic forces of modern history and technology,
MacLennan no longer believed "human destiny" was the product of
individual human action ("Story" 36-37). But he also wanted to affirm the
worth of human existence in a theodicy of "good, evil and the possibility of
justifying God's ways to man" (qtd. in E. Cameron, *Life* 280). Since "the
basic human conflict" is spiritual, therefore, he decided to "write a book
which would not depend on character-in-action, but on spirit-in-action. The
conflict here, the essential one, was between the human spirit of Everyman
and Everyman's human condition" of mortality and potential
meaninglessness. To find "an accurate fictional form for this concept of life"
he laboured for six years: "I refined my style and discovered new techniques I
had previously known nothing about" ("Story" 37).

As many critics have pointed out, his "new techniques" are hardly
original decades after Joyce, Woolf, and Faulkner. However, Elspeth
Cameron explains that, far from being ignorant of modern fictional
developments, MacLennan had experimented with "stream of consciousness"
in his first unpublished novel, "So All Their Praises" (1933) and deliberately
discarded it because "while stream-of-consciousness could certainly show
'within' the individual, it could not portray simultaneously 'the human
condition'. . . . Furthermore, the breakdown of structured language seemed to
him to undermine that 'affirmation of life' he believed to be 'the supreme
function of art'" (*Life* 276). However, the change from third person
omniscient to first person narrative and a complex flashback structure made
this novel more organically "character-centred" than his previous ones. These
technical advances helped him solve the perennial problem for a religious
writer, which arises most acutely in this, his most ambitious book: how,
realistically, to portray faith in fiction, the action of grace in nature. Although
the theme is the spiritual dilemma of the modern world, and the setting spans
the century and the globe in its allusions, this novel is most powerfully
convincing as the personal religious quest of George Stewart.

Much of the emotional power of the novel is due to the autobiographical similarities between George Stewart and the author: a writer and university professor, scarred by the Depression and a schoolmastering job, now living in Montreal with a wife who is dying of a rheumatic heart condition (as Dorothy MacLennan did in 1957). After the fact, MacLennan saw the archetypal power of his real-life experience transmitted "through art": "We lived . . . the conflux of the two basic myths of the human race: death and resurrection, both of which revert to the prehistoric origins of original sin" (qtd. in E. Cameron, *Life* 280). Consequently, George also represents the Everyman of "a generation which yearned to belong, so unsuccessfully, to something larger than themselves" (*WE* 4). This articulation of the religious theme of the book recalls William James's definition of "religious experience": "that we can experience union with *something* larger than ourselves and in that union find our greatest peace" (*WE* 499). The search for peace — a truce between man's spirit and his fate — is the premise and substance of *The Watch That Ends the Night*.

Beginning in Montreal in February 1951, George leads the reader gently into a series of flashbacks which span four decades before returning to the present. And, in a pattern repeated throughout the novel, he prepares us theologically for the events he then dramatizes. He tells us that as a boy he had been religious and believed in a personal, living God. Unlike MacLennan's other heroes, George did not suffer the repressions of a strict Calvinist upbringing. Nevertheless, in the disillusionments of the thirties, like millions of others, he lost his faith in religion, in himself, and in the integrity of human society (*WE* 107). And the manifest injustices of the world, symbolized for him in his wife's illness, have increased his rejection of any divine Power (*WE* 6). So, in the hubristic, self-centred fifties he finds his religion, his "rock" and his "salvation" in the palpably mortal life and love of Catherine. As Goetsch has pointed out, "George belongs to the stock type of naive narrator," and MacLennan is deftly preparing us to see his rash confidence (covering a basically insecure nature) corrected by the passage of time and new religious insights (26-27).

Catherine Carey-Martell-Stewart represents a quasi-divine "spiritual force" in George's life. She is primarily characterized by the "Life-Force" which has developed in her in response to her lifelong struggle against her "fate" which is her rheumatic heart. Therefore, in words which MacLennan later borrowed for "The Story of a Novel," George says that this spirit has become for him "the ultimate reality": "I think of this story not as one conditioned by character, as the dramatists understand it, but by the spirit and the human condition" (*WE* 25). And this spirit is "the sole force which equals the merciless fate which binds a human being to his mortality" (*WE* 26, cf. 341). It is her strength and her knowledge that "all loving is a loving of life in the midst of death" (*WE* 69) that George leans on for years until he is forced to develop his own spiritual resources.

Among George's generation, in which "so many of the successful ones, after trying desperately to hitch their wagons to some great belief, ended up believing in nothing but their own cleverness" (*WE* 101), towers the mythological figure of Jerome Martell, Catherine's first husband and George's spiritual father. He too is larger than life, another brilliant doctor, "more like a force of nature than a man" (*WE* 150). In Part V of the novel MacLennan recreates Jerome's heroic story. An illegitimate orphan, he escapes from his mother's murderer in a New Brunswick logging camp, and is finally adopted by a devoutly religious clergyman and his wife in Halifax. His life has the symbolic dimension of a modern *Pilgrim's Progress*; we are told that during his youth "he had really thought of himself as a soldier of God. He believed the Gospels literally, and they meant far more to him than they could mean to most people, because he had such a desperate need to belong" (*WE* 215-16). But the horror and guilt of World War I destroyed his religion, forcing him to seek absolution in medicine and politics for the senseless killing.

For George he epitomizes the anguished decade of the thirties:

> This was a time in which you were always meeting people who caught politics just as a person catches religion. It was probably the last time in this century when politics in our country will be evangelical, and if a man was once intensely religious, he was bound to be wide open to a mood like that of the Thirties. (*WE* 223-24)

Jerome is one of many who divert the passions that no longer serve a traditional God into this neo-religious faith. Having failed to fill "the vacuum left by his lost religion" with Catherine's human love (*WE* 239), he seeks salvation through humanistic works:

> I used to dream of a city on top of a hill — Athens perhaps. It was white and it was beautiful, and it was a great privilege to enter it. I used to dream that if I worked hard all my life, and tried hard all my life, maybe some day I'd be allowed within its gates. And now I see the fascists besieging that city. . . . (*WE* 244-45)

Confronted by the spectre of Original Sin in capitalist medicine and fascist politics, Jerome embarks on a crusade to save mankind. But he is all too aware that his City of Civilization on top of a hill is a substitute for Bunyan's Celestial City, and Augustine's City of God, as he articulates half of the theme of this novel:

> A man must belong to something larger than himself. He must surrender to it. God was so convenient for that purpose when people could believe in Him. He was so safe and so remote. . . . Now there is nothing but people. . . . The only immortality is mankind. (*WE* 270-72)

Jerome, therefore, having seen his "light on the road to Damascus" (*WE* 264), leaves his family to serve in the Spanish Civil War like "a divine fool" (*WE* 297).

Years later, after he is reported tortured and killed by the Nazis, George and Catherine marry and a new era begins. In the forties and fifties they search for meaning and purpose in a world from which "the Lord who had shepherded Israel and our fathers had gone away and we had lost the habit of searching for Him" (*WE* 285). With the various political gods of the thirties discredited, their generation gradually sells out their ideals in exchange for personal peace and affluence. And the "larger thing" that most people belong to is the nuclear family:

> In the Thirties all of us who were young had been united by anger and the obviousness of our plight; in the war we had been united by fear and the obviousness of the danger. But now, prosperous under the bomb, we all seemed to have become atomized. . . . The gods, false or true, had vanished. The bell which only a few years ago had tolled for us all, now tolled for each family in its prosperous solitude. (*WE* 323)

After two embolisms (like two World Wars), Catherine's life symbolizes the world in the fifties, living "under the bomb." George desperately clings to her, as her spirit comes to represent "the container of a life-force resisting extinction" (*WE* 324), in a vain confidence that she will render him impervious to his fate.

It is at this point that Jerome Martell returns from the dead, in the manner of Christ, to witness to the second half of the theme: what every man "requires to know and feel if he is to live with a sense of how utterly tremendous is the mystery our ancestors confidently called God" (*WE* 324). He has had a vision of Jesus in his prison cell: "He wasn't the Jesus of the churches. He wasn't the Jesus who had died for our sins. He was simply a man who had died and risen again. Who had died outwardly as I had died inwardly" (*WE* 330). It is this vision that has given him the courage to affirm the value of life in the face of death.

Part VII of the novel illustrates most clearly the difficulty of expressing and dramatizing a religious vision within the dynamics of a realistic narrative. George describes his agony when Catherine suffers her third embolism. The deep sincerity and intense feeling of this section are, no doubt, partly autobiographical. Many of the details are similar to MacLennan's memories of his wife's illness, recorded in his essays "Christmas without Dickens" (*TT* 112-23) and "Victory" (*OS* 177-83). Significantly, these both end in powerful religious affirmations:

> The body was seeking its own dissolution, but the spirit it carried was nearing clarity. Through this experience became manifest some of those

mysterious things spoken of in the last chapters of St. John's Gospel, and I
knew they were true. (*OS* 183)

As David Staines suggests, the emotional power of the novel's ending may
reside in the literary transformation of this autobiography into elegy
("Commentary" 67).

When George is first confronted with Catherine's merciless fate, he
reacts as Everyman, subconsciously revolting against the emptiness of
existence: "For to be equal to fate is to be equal to the knowledge that
everything we have done, achieved, endured and been proud and ashamed of
is nothing" (*WE* 340). In a theological interlude in Chapter iv, George
explains man's need for a god and the insufficiency and impermanence of all
the various substitutes: reason, ability, success, wife and family, political
systems and the state. When they fail, he is prey to the "Great Fear," the
existential anxiety that God is indifferent and life is meaningless, and this
threatens to obliterate his identity in the destructive terrors of the chaotic
subconscious (*WE* 341-42). Then, using the words of Scripture — "let there
be light" (Gen. 1:2-3) — and the analogies of music — the melodies of Bach
and Beethoven — he attempts to describe the spiritual experience that finally
resolves "the final human struggle" between the "light and dark within the
soul" into an ultimate harmony (paraphrasing I Corinthians 13:7): ". . . which
is a will to live, love, grow and be grateful, the determination to endure all
things, suffer all things, hope all things, believe all things necessary for what
our ancestors called the glory of God" (*WE* 343-44). This union of the spirit
of Everyman with the "Unknowable which at that instant makes available His
power, and for that instant existing, becomes known" (*WE* 344) is, in
theological terms, "mysticism" (*Oxford Dictionary of the Christian Church*).
It is this "mystical approach to a vision of God" which MacLennan has
invoked in his essays as a new theology of mediation (*CC* 153). This vision
defeats the modern death wish, vindicates God to scientific man, justifies the
human plight, and celebrates life: "[I]t is of no importance that God appears
indifferent to justice as men understand it. He gave life. He gave it. Life for
a year, a month, a day or an hour is still a gift" (*WE* 344).

In the final chapters of the novel, MacLennan attempts to dramatize
this theology in his fiction. George's subconscious revolts against Catherine's
suffering in a hatred of life, self, and others, and an utter hopelessness that
MacLennan universalizes as "the world living under the bomb" (*WE* 364).
However, as Jerome explains the mystical experience (which both he and
Catherine have had) of dying to self in order to live again without fear
(*WE* 365-66), George comes to a new self-knowledge and acceptance of
life:

All of us is Everyman and this is intolerable unless each of us can also be
I. . . . Behind me I heard Jerome say: "Jesus said, 'I am the resurrection

and the life.' He died in order to prove it and he rose in order to prove it. His spirit rose. He died in order to live. If He had not died, He would not have lived." (*WE* 367-68)

With images of light, music, cleansing, and rebirth, George's spirit affirms the worth and the continuity of life that would not end with death but "would be translated into the mysterious directions of the spirit which breathed upon the void" (*WE* 370).

The Epilogue is George's benediction on a life lived under the bomb but in the spirit, waiting for Catherine's death. They have learned that "the final and only sanction of human existence" is not political, material, or social, but spiritual:

All our lives we had wanted to belong to something larger than ourselves. We belonged consciously to nothing now except to the pattern of our lives and fates. To God, possibly. I am chary of using that much-misused word, but I say honestly that at least I was conscious of His power. Whatever the spirit might be I did not know, but I knew it was there. (*WE* 372)

The purpose and value of life are found at the end of "the watch that ends the night" (as, symbolically, Psalm 90 is used in the Requiem Mass). To the "good and faithful servant" will come the invitation, "Enter thou into the joy of the Lord," and the benediction, "*nunc requiescas in perpetuum*" (*WE* 373).

Again, I think this novel can be illuminated by reference to Paul Tillich's theology. When Jerome Martell's "courage to be as a part" and George Stewart's "courage to be as oneself" are ultimately discredited as faiths for the twentieth century, MacLennan turns to "the courage to be" for a theological solution. The inner harmony and death to self which George arrives at is an experience of "mysticism," defined by Tillich as "the striving for union with ultimate reality, and the corresponding courage to take the non-being which is implied in finitude upon oneself" (*Courage* 156). However, "the courage to be in its radical form is a key to an idea of God which transcends both mysticism and the person-to-person encounter" of traditional theism (*Courage* 173). George's final affirmation of life is "the self-affirmation of being-itself": "There are no valid arguments for the 'existence' of God, but there are acts of courage in which we affirm the power of being. . . . Courage has revealing power, the courage to be is the key to being-itself" (*Courage* 175-76).

Most significantly, MacLennan recognizes that the ground of being must include non-being within it:

This, which is darkness, also is light. This, which is no, also is yes. This, which is hatred, also is love. This, which is fear, also is courage. This, which is defeat, also is victory. Who knows the things of the spirit except the spirit of man which is within him? said St. Paul. (*WE* 344)

Tillich said the same thing in *The Courage to Be* (173-75), and in *Religionsphilosophie der Kultur* (proving that MacLennan was right — the musicians' version is briefer and better):

> Religion is an experience of the Unconditioned and that means an experience of absolute reality on the ground of the experience of absolute nothingness; it will experience the nothingness of all existing things, the nothingness of values, the nothingness of the personal life, where this experience has led to the absolute, radical No, there it shifts into an equally absolute experience of reality, into a radical Yes. (trans. and qtd. in Adams 43)

MacLennan's theology is profound and Protestant; it arises out of the despair of the existential situation, not from an imposed orthodoxy. *The Watch That Ends the Night* is the prime example of the paradox in MacLennan's writing: the conflict between faith and fiction — between the ideas and the art — is nevertheless responsible for the scope and significance of his novels. Critics agree on the importance and clarity of the theme of this novel, and on the sincerity and intensity of feeling which give it such persuasive power. The problem, as always, is to dramatize the faith in terms of realistic fiction. MacLennan's choice of a first-person narrator is crucial: George Stewart is usually a likeable, intelligent and convincing narrator. Since his voice, character, and occupation (history teacher and commentator) are well established and naturally close to MacLennan's, the inevitable didactic interludes seem less authorial and much better integrated into the characterization than in previous novels.

As we have seen, the characters of Catherine and Jerome are almost purely symbolic and of mythic dimensions, and many critics have argued that they are unconvincing in realistic fiction. However, MacLennan has carefully pointed out that this is a story of "spirit-in-action," not "character-in-action." In the context of George Stewart's first-person spiritual quest, they are effective as representatives of psychological realities (Goetsch sees them as Jungian archetypes [26-27]) and of spiritual states.

The plot is generally a product of the character development of the hero; even the amazing return of Jerome, since it is presented as the premise of the plot, and the complex flashback structure do not appear as contrived as the endings of MacLennan's previous novels. The various stages of George's life are vividly documented in dramatic set-pieces: with his family, at Waterloo School, in the academic gatherings and political meetings of the thirties, in the CBC and on assignment, at the university, and finally at the hospital. The most memorable and longest sequence is Part V of the book, Jerome's flight from the wilderness in a canoe, a brilliant action narrative which becomes a natural objective correlative for George's existential fear in the rest of the story. MacLennan's descriptions of Montreal during the Depression are especially vivid: the setting and social analysis give the city character-status. As usual, the supporting actors are admirably drawn, from the satiric caricatures (Dr. Bigbee, Shatwell, Adam Blore, etc.) to the sympathetic bystanders (Jack Christopher, Sally and many more, including nurses and taxi drivers), all of whom come to life movingly on the page. Their dialogue is usually realistic; it is the passages of deep emotion among the central characters, and especially the treatment of sexual love, that are so embarrassingly false.

Part VII, of course, has given the critics the most difficulty with its "sermon-like peroration" (Lucas 42). As MacLennan admits in the novel, nobody has ever described this spiritual struggle truly "in words" (*WE* 343). Therefore, he is forced to use analogy, imagery, even bald rhetoric to convey the experience. There is much deeply moving drama, character conflict, and psychological realism in this section. Nevertheless, the ending is not wholly successful because it is basically non-dramatic. It transposes the existential problem into religious subjectivity and metaphysical idealism. When the world surrounding George becomes "a shadow" (*WE* 373), it is no longer the subject of realistic fiction.

This lack of realism is partly a result of MacLennan's abstract theological model. In adopting a Tillichian concept of God, he answered the existential needs of modern agnosticism, but he stripped the divine of the objective personal qualities which have characterized Judeo-Christian theology and traditional portrayals of religious experience (cf. *Courage* 177). Therefore MacLennan's catalogue of theistic attributes in the final section of *The Watch That Ends the Night* — "humanity's supreme invention" "revealed in a mystery of the feelings" (344); "the mystery" and "pattern" and "spirit" of life and nature (372) — portrays a subjective philosophical hypothesis but precludes a dramatic personal relationship.

7. *Return of the Sphinx*

In *Return of the Sphinx* (1967) MacLennan did not repeat the basic techniques, or the success, of *The Watch That Ends the Night*. This novel replays the conflict between the races and generations which we saw in *Two Solitudes*, but two decades later MacLennan's basic optimism has given way to an elegy for lost idealism. The lesson here is that history is cyclical and every generation must repeat the religious quest of the modern world: from the death of God, through false ideologies, to spiritual grace. MacLennan now realized that the blunderings of his contemporaries, although they were "one of the supreme betraying generations" (D. Cameron, "MacLennan" 135) were by no means unique. The sins of the fathers have been visited on the third and fourth generations, and the postwar children he thought so much "freer in their souls" (*WE* 4) in fact still have to wrestle with the existential human condition.

The conflict between the hero Alan Ainslie and his son Daniel is a microcosm not only of the separatist struggle in Quebec, but of the moral, spiritual, and humanistic disintegration of the second half of the twentieth century. As many critics have noted, MacLennan's characterization is based on archetypes, and in *Return of the Sphinx* all the major characters are again orphans. They represent mankind, bereft of faith in a divine Father, wandering a world uprooted by the political and economic cataclysms of this modern era, searching for peace and love. False political gods originate in this desire to "belong," this "love-hunger growing imperceptibly into hunger for power" (*RS* 7).

MacLennan's biographer has demonstrated how deeply he was influenced during the writing of this novel by G. Rattray Taylor's *Sex in History*, an application of Freudian theories (especially the Oedipus complex) to the cycles of history (E. Cameron, *Life* 314-16). He borrowed Taylor's analysis that the modern world has moved from a "patrist" (authoritarian) to a "matrist" (permissive) society as the sociological basis for his novel, and explained this in an article written shortly after its publication. In the process of changing from the old Victorian "patrist" order to a "matrist" one, society has destroyed "the validity of the Father," both divine and secular, institutional and personal: "the idea accepted throughout history that the word 'father' implies trust, reliability, a certain valiancy, a deserved authority and continued respect when he is old" ("Reflections" 35).

The real story of *Return of the Sphinx* is not separatism but "the revolt of Youth" against the "really tough parental authority" of the Roman Catholic Church in Quebec, symbolized in "the destruction of a well-meaning father by an unhappy, ambitious, confused, guilt-ridden, idealistic son" ("Reflections" 36-37). However, since "no individual, much less a large percentage of an ethnic population, can abandon a religion as strong as Catholicism without feeling a terrible loss" (*RS* 298), spiritual aspirations have been converted into political ideals. Robin Mathews rightly points out that MacLennan "refuses to make any serious analysis of economic, political and class conflict in Quebec" in this novel ("Nationalist" 63). On the contrary, he is concerned with a deeper and more universal pattern of existential conflict and religious quests. Politics are portrayed as the byproduct of spiritual yearnings and sexual/generational conflicts, symbolized by the eponymous sphinx which refers to the myth MacLennan used as the basis of the book: *Oedipus at Colonus* (E. Cameron, *Life* 319).

The hero Alan Ainslie is the grown-up Alan MacNeil of *Each Man's Son*. His foster father has brought him up without any religion at all in order to protect him from Calvinist superstition. As a result, he is "by nature . . . a religious man" (*RS* 96) who "believes in God but won't go to church" (*RS* 42). This vague deism has given him no refuge or consolation after the senseless death of his wife Constance, who (like Catherine Stewart) was "the governor of his life's engine" (*RS* 76), and his real "salvation" (*RS* 28). Nor does his commitment to humanism and civilization, first at the United Nations and then in Canadian federalism, ultimately replace religion and earn him a sense of justification and salvation. As his daughter Chantal explains (in an echo of Jerome Martell):

> That old father of his — he gave Dad the idea that his life ought to be some kind of Pilgrim's Progress to some kind of City of God and what did Dad turn *that* into? His City of God is this greedy country that rewards every bastard who milks it, and breaks the heart of everyone who loves it. . . . (*RS* 43)

When we meet Ainslie, his earthly gods — expressed in the same images as those of George Stewart and Jerome Martell — have suffered the same fate as theirs. His book, *The Death of a Victorian*, is, like this novel, an elegy for lost idealism, another requiem for the well-meaning generation:

> The time he was living in was too fantastic for anyone to look it square in the eye. Hurricane weather but no hurricanes. Nuclear confrontations with serious-minded men seriously wondering whether there would be even a blade of grass left on the planet inside a few years, but so far no bombs. Full employment but no security. Knowledge in unknowable quantities but never so many people telling each other they could not understand. All the ideas that had guided and inspired Ainslie's life — socialism, education, the faith that science and prosperity would improve man's life, even the new psychology which everyone so glibly talked — the best he could say now of any of these hopes was that they had foundered in the ancient ocean of human nature. (*RS* 74-75)

Ainslie's only remaining hope seems as doomed, from the beginning of this novel, as all the others: "If Canada can hold together, she could become a pilot plant for a new kind of nation and a new kind of freedom" (*RS* 256).

His son Daniel is part of the new generation that is repeating the mistakes of the past: "That sort of talk sounds so excruciatingly reminiscent of students in the 30s . . ." (*RS* 49-50). After a deeply "religious phase" in which he attended a seminary, Daniel has "lost his religion along with most of the rest of them his age" (*RS* 49). Emotionally orphaned by the death of his mother, estranged from his father to whom he had never been close, he seeks his identity and purpose in "The Movement." As Joe Lacombe explains, this revolt of Quebec youth against the traditional faith, parental authority, and the patriarchal church is motivated by desires for sexual freedom, material success, and political power — all the secular gods of The System (*RS* 103-5). But ironically, when the security of the church has been removed, there was "no comfort left for the youth of the world. . . . The System had taken it away" (*RS* 189). Thus, nationalism or separatism becomes their "surrogate religion." Ainslie recognizes this situation:

[N]o people in history has ever tried to break with a strict Catholicism without turning to nationalism or some other kind of ism as a surrogate religion. As I see it, that is the essence of the situation in Quebec today. The problem there isn't economic, it's psychological. . . . It's a genuine revolution in a way of life, and I don't have to remind you that all revolutions have neurotic roots. (*RS* 69)

It is the neurosis that MacLennan is chiefly examining. The refuge from a lost religion was politics for Jerome Martel and sex for Stephen Lassiter; it is both for Daniel Ainslie. Despite Daniel's ideological rhetoric in support of The Movement and against The System (which is the American "Way of Life" and economic imperialism [*RS* 145]), it is made clear that his motives are basically self-seeking (symbolized by the technological/ phallic power of his television show and his sports car). Daniel finds self-justification, existential meaning, and a hope for material independence and power in the separatist movement, as well as a father-figure in Aimé Latendresse who is, significantly, a "spoiled priest" (*RS* 145). With new confidence he also finds a sexual outlet and, in an Oedipal triumph, a surrogate mother in Marielle. But his youthful rebellion and his sexual liberation are in conflict with his puritanical religious upbringing: "Fornication is at once both a disease and a habit. . . . it damages the body and ruins the soul" (*RS* 180). So he sublimates his guilt and converts his religious longing into a dream of being a secular redeemer: "Now he knew he had to liberate this nation even if it involved his own death. He heard his name mentioned with reverence by thankful people long after he was gone, as the Christians spoke the names of their martyrs" (*RS* 182).

MacLennan places Daniel's motivation in the context of his universal theme when Ainslie explains separatist terrorism as a symptom of a world that has lost its faith in both theology and humanism:

I believe the crisis came when humanity lost its faith in man's ability to improve his own nature. . . . When people no longer can believe in personal immortality, when society at large has abandoned philosophy, many men grow desperate without knowing why. . . . Some of them will do *anything* — no matter how hopeless, criminal or idiotic — merely to have people mention their names and recognize that they exist. . . . A senseless crime can be one way of passing into the only kind of immortality this sick epoch understands, and so can the leadership of a senseless revolt. . . . (*RS* 267)

The generation gap between Ainslie and Daniel explodes into an Oedipal confrontation when the father discovers Daniel and Marielle in his marriage bed, and results in the prophesied violent and "senseless crime" which destroys Ainslie's political mission for federalism. When the son is jailed, the father withdraws into himself and his love of the country for solace. In the Epilogue of the novel Ainslie makes a cross-Canada pilgrimage, then returns to his Laurentian retreat to celebrate a wedding in happy fellowship with his French-Canadian neighbours. He also meditates on the impending wedding of Chantal and his best friend Gabriel Fleury, a marriage which symbolizes, in addition to the peaceful union of English and French (as in *Two Solitudes*), also the harmony of the New World and the Old, youth and age.

At the end Ainslie finds a philosophic hope in the "vast land. Too vast even for fools to ruin all of it," and in the cycle of history: "The sphinx has returned to the world before, after all" (*RS* 303). However, his vague, pantheistic optimism concerning the value and meaning of life lacks the theological resolution of *The Watch That Ends the Night*:

> Looking over the lake he at last accepted that he had merely happened into all this. Constance, Chantal, Daniel, Gabriel — they and all the others had merely happened into this loveliness that nobody could understand or possess, and that some tried to control or destroy just because they were unable to possess or understand it. Merely happened into this joy and pain and movement of limbs, of hope, fear, shame and the rest of it, the little chipmunk triumphs and defeats. He believed it would endure. He thanked God he had been of it, was of it. (*RS* 303)

The theology at the end of this novel can be seen as a logical development of MacLennan's emphasis on the subjective, mystical experience of God, most often associated with nature, as in the Epilogue to *The Watch That Ends the Night*. "Mysticism, with its passionate search for God in nature and desire for union with the Divine, has often verged on pantheism" (*Oxford Dictionary of the Christian Church*). Ainslie's pantheistic providence embraces humanity in a divine pattern which MacLennan explained to his editor in 1967 as: ". . . the hand of the Lord. In modern times, it's the built-in instinct of self-preservation within a living species" (qtd. in E. Cameron, *Life* 337). In response to the failure of traditional religion to answer the existential anxieties of our time, MacLennan reinterpreted the God of his ancestors, in accordance with modern liberal theology, as a psychological and scientific hypothesis inherent in humanity and nature — what he later termed "the God of evolution." In this redefinition, he followed the spirit of New Theology:

> When "providence" has become a superstition and "immortality" something imaginary, that which once was the power in these symbols can still be present and create the courage to be in spite of the experience of a chaotic world and a finite existence. . . . When "divine judgment" is interpreted as a psychological complex and forgiveness as a remnant of the "father-image, what once was the power in those symbols can still be present and create the courage to be in spite of the experience of an infinite gap between what we are and what we ought to be. . . . The courage to be is

rooted in the God who appears when God has disappeared in the anxiety of doubt. (Tillich, *Courage* 183)

However, the problem with the Epilogue of *Return of the Sphinx* is not that it is unorthodox Christianity, but that it is in artistic opposition to the rest of the novel. Throughout the book MacLennan has honestly dramatized the despair of modern society in the escalating conflict between father and son. The violent confrontations at the end of the story are a logical development of the central dramatic situation. But the Epilogue is a facile, metaphysical negation of the atmosphere and implications of the entire novel. In it MacLennan seems impelled to offer his religious vision of the grace operating in nature that he has not realistically been able to dramatize in his plot: the hope in Providence ("God Himself may have sent Joe Lacombe after [Daniel] that night") that is subverted by his simultaneous image of tragic determinism ("the stars, too, were trapped in equations" [*RS* 307]).

There are other weaknesses in the craftsmanship of this novel. The sociopolitical analysis is a simplistic generalization. MacLennan again loads his characters with rhetorical digressions on many of his pet concerns: modern education, sexual licence, city architecture, modern technology, American imperialism and multinational corporations, and the traumas of his generation. Moreover, there are too many characters with too many personal stories, interesting and instructive in themselves, but distracting from the principal conflict. And the main characters are too didactically allegorical. For example, Ainslie's face is split like Canada and "he's got the fence right in his crotch" (*RS* 113). His marriage to Constance symbolized federalism, but she was destroyed by impossible technology and consumerism (a processed-cheese truck with faulty brakes). Ainslie, Daniel and Gabriel, archetypally, all spend their lives trying to run away from the first sight of their fathers.

The "schizophrenic form" of the narration is a result of the misplaced prominence of Gabriel Fleury, originally the narrator (in early drafts) but finally only a minor symbol and authorial chorus (E. Cameron, *Life* 318-19). MacLennan's decision to return from the successful first person narrative of *The Watch That Ends the Night* to a detached third person voice with multiple centres of consciousness was intended to highlight the hero, Alan Ainslie, but he does not focus on him soon enough or often enough. Consequently, the central conflict, especially in Book One, is lost in a jumble of other narratives and flashbacks, and a proliferation of times and places. Book Two has a much tighter action and build-up of suspense, but even here there are unexplained inconsistencies and dead-end digressions (for example, Ainslie's story about Archie MacNeil and Daniel's subsequent investigation of him — presumably an attempt to establish a genetic link for Daniel's violence). Thus, the ultimate transposition of the tragic events of Book Two into "little chipmunk triumphs and defeats" transcended by the abstract theological optimism of the Epilogue, seems the final subversion of the plot, a triumph of dogma over drama.

8. *Voices in Time*

Thirteen years after *Return of the Sphinx* MacLennan published *Voices in Time* (1980) at the age of seventy-three, a final elegy for the present but with surprising hope for the future. The novel is set in a dystopian future, about 2039 (*VT* 170), but despite a brief science fiction beginning, it makes no pretence to be a futurist novel. The perspective is established so that the novelist (through his seventy-five-year-old narrator) can reflect back with apocalyptic omniscience on the tragedies of the twentieth century, including our present age: "I had no wish whatever to write futuristically. . . . fiction requires a perspective in time and now there is no perspective because the changes are coming so fast" (qtd. in E. Cameron, *Life* 355). This perspective allows the historian MacLennan to view the cycles of civilization: the repetition of the errors of the 1930s in the 1960s, and the eventual "self-murder of a civilization" (*VT* 249) in the 1990s through the logical development of irresponsible technology and materialism, coupled with moral and spiritual decadence. The portrait of decay recalls his analysis of the fall of the Roman Empire in his doctoral dissertation, *Oxyrhynchus*. The hope that illuminates all these historical disasters (even his prophetic Armageddon) lies in the cyclical renewal of humanity after each self-destructive tragedy.

At first glance, *Voices in Time* may not seem as thematically religious as his two previous novels, since there are fewer overt references to traditional theology in the novel. However, as MacLennan's essays and interviews make clear, and his biographer has fully documented, the philosophical framework of the book is based on his religious answer for humanity and the final development of his new theology, his modern vision of God.

In 1969 MacLennan discovered Robert Ardry's theories of the New Biology, and Ardrey's "views of the evolution of man provided a convenient mythology to which [MacLennan] could link his already evolutionary view of the life process" (E. Cameron, *Life* 347). In all his novels MacLennan has portrayed the human duality of creative and destructive forces: divine immanence and original sin are natural concepts for a Calvinist. In a 1970 essay he indicated how far he had come from the political and humanist solutions of his earliest novels: "Man's real troubles are not caused by political and economic systems and only incidentally by scoundrels, but by the cruel contradictions planted in his nature by no less an authority than the God of Evolution Himself" (*CC* viii). Nevertheless, in the face of the suicidal destruction of humanity by its own modern technology and political upheavals, he posits a hope in this God of Evolution who wills the cyclical renewal of the human race: "I happen to believe in the God that's implicit in evolution, . . . this is part of the chain of life, as I see it. It's away above politics. . . . I think our ancestors would call it divine when they said that God is not mocked" (D. Cameron, "MacLennan" 132). After the 1970 October Crisis in Quebec, MacLennan applied his radical redefinition of traditional theism to the nuclear age:

> Underneath it all of course is the mid-20th century volcano, its causes so mysterious I am convinced they are lodged in the evolutionary process itself. What some New Biologists have called "The Keeper of the Kinds" permits no species to threaten the survival of all species, including itself, and this is what our military technocrats have been doing with gusto for more than 20 years, with promise of more to come. ("Quebec Crisis" 17)

In *Voices in Time* MacLennan laments the sin that destroys humanity despite much grace and goodness, and celebrates the hope of the resurrection in the rebuilding of civilization. John Wellfleet, MacLennan's principal spokesman in the novel, reconstructs the twentieth century from the "voices in time" (*VT* 27) which come to him in a box from the past delivered by André Gervais, an architect of the future. Although we get bits of John's personal story, he functions primarily as historical expositor and channel for the stories of his stepfather, Conrad Dehmel, and older cousin, Timothy Wellfleet. These older relatives were tragically caught up as actors/victims in the socio-political maelstroms of the thirties and the sixties, before the final Great Fear (nuclear blackmail) and Destructions (global annihilation by "clean bombs") which John experienced in the nineties. The parallels between these three men, approximately three decades apart, illustrate MacLennan's theme of the evolution of history, particularly the patrist-matrist cycles of Nazi Germany (patrist) and FLQ Quebec (matrist) that we have seen previewed in *The Watch That Ends the Night* and *Return of the Sphinx*.

The connection between Conrad's era and Timothy's is the factor that links them back to the fall of the Roman Empire (cf. *OS* 282 and *CC* 140) and forward to the spiritual sterility of MacLennan's fictional twenty-first century (*VT* 170): the loss of religion and society's consequent substitutions. Conrad explains:

> After the 1914 war, religion died out among millions of young Germans. This left a void in their lives and many turned to nationalism as a substitute for the religion they had lost. In the 1960s, religion also died out among the young all over the world and nationalisms of every kind are taking its place. (*VT* 115)

The patrist era of the thirties and two world wars produced the matrist reaction portrayed in *Return of the Sphinx*. We are now told that the sixties permissiveness eventually resulted in a patrist backlash just before the Destructions and during the decades of the Bureaucracies after that cataclysm. André Gervais now lives in an authoritarian, repressive era; in order to rebuild society and avoid repeating the errors of the past, he must learn about its history from John.

However, a mature MacLennan — less idealistic than in his early humanist novels — now knows there may be no Santayana solution for the fateful repetitions of history and no secular answer to Gervais's question about the creative versus destructive forces in humanity: "But if there were men with all that knowledge, why couldn't they stop what happened?" (*VT* 13). For, as John realizes in a retrospective on Hitler's Final Solution: "trained men of reason are the last to recognize the bared teeth of the human ape when it appears before them. Half a century later, when I was young, it was the same story all over again" (*VT* 178). The ultimate answer is theological not humanistic. Conrad Dehmel gives MacLennan's analysis of life as another wise old man:

> In the relatively rare periods in the past that we call civilized, people understood that a civilization is like a garden cultivated in a jungle. As flowers and vegetables grow from cultivated seeds, so do civilizations grow from carefully studied, diligently examined ideas and perceptions In nature, if there are no gardeners, the weeds that need no cultivation take over the garden and destroy it. . . . During my lifetime too many of the men who thought of themselves as civilization's gardeners, in nearly everything they did from the promotion of superhuman science to superhuman salesmanship, devoted the ambiguous genius of their programmed brains to the cultivation of the weeds. They watered them with the jungle rains of the media. The klieg lights of the studios were their hothouses. They did what they did, and they still do it, with the best of intentions, because they cannot believe that the creative energy of the universe will never interfere with human ingenuity. If anyone said to them, "Thou shalt have no other gods before me," they would reply with a polite and pitying smile. (*VT* 121-22)

However, individual human tragedy will still not be averted, in spite of this theology that the "creative energy of the universe" (the God of Evolution, the Keeper of the Kinds) will save destructive "human ingenuity" from completely annihilating itself. Dehmel, the good but naive man, witnesses the betrayal and destruction of his parents, his Jewish lover and her family, and his own intellectual and physical integrity by the "jungle" of Nazi Germany. Finally, he is killed by the modern media "klieg lights" represented by the technologically irresponsible, power-corrupted Timothy Wellfleet. Nevertheless, the human race is preserved from complete devastation by their irresponsible inventiveness by "something profound and mysterious, something blessed and almighty in the genes of humanity" (*VT* 247). And there is hope that wise people like Dehmel and John Wellfleet (and MacLennan) may be able to pass on the lessons of the garden. Appalled by "Hitler's Germany," Dehmel (sounding more like the defeated Alan Ainslie than the pugnacious Jerome Martell) vows: "My old dream of earning the right to belong to civilization as its interpreter vanished. What was needed now was not to belong to the old civilization, but to survive this nihilism in order to preserve the seeds of a new civilization" (*VT* 207). Similarly, John's attempt to transmit "the seeds" to André Gervais signals a hope for future generations in the return of salmon to the St. Lawrence (*VT* 24), the rediscovery of culture and "moral philosophy" (*VT* 122), and the rebuilding of cities in a "second Renaissance" unthreatened by "the technological system that destroyed them" (*VT* 124). As John says in the first lines of his book recording these "voices in time":

> As it is with the individual, so it may be with the whole world. When the individual is wounded in his soul he often wishes to die. But time passes and then, for no reason he understands, he wants to live again. Can it be the same with communities? (*VT* 28)

The complex structure of this novel encloses flashbacks within flashbacks, voices within voices, to achieve elaborate comparisons and contrasts between periods and characters within the historical and theological overview I have sketched. Conrad Dehmel's story is the longest (over half of the book and five of the ten chapters) and most compelling. The most admirable character, he represents the ideal of German culture and intellect corrupted and destroyed in two world wars by automatic obedience to the father, the Fatherland and Hitler who was the personification of "the preposterous German authoritarian superego that demands more of people than any individual can fulfil" (*VT* 176). Symbolically, the patrist forces, represented by Conrad's well-meaning but discipline-driven father, crush the gentle cultural influences of Conrad's mother and maternal grandfather and destroy his world.

In diametrical opposition to Conrad, the naive victim who becomes an ineffectual opponent of the patrist-repressive regime, is Timothy Wellfleet, the street-smart villain and self-deluded personification of the matrist-permissive sixties. In his story (one third of the book in two chapters), Timothy is portrayed as an illiterate, pop-culture icon. He stars in a superficial, exploitative television programme named for a temporary sexual orgasm ("This is Now" [*VT* 65]) and dedicated to destroying the establishment. The rebellious son of an immoral, abdicating mother and a confused, authoritarian father whose values have been perverted into guilty indulgence, Timothy is a child of the times:

> How could anyone be a human being in that decade of the spiritual castrati programmed by Dr. Spock, interpreted by the interpreters of Dr. Freud, its religion packaged in cellophane by Doctors Peale, Sheen, and Graham, the whole lot of them conned into believing, into really believing, that nobody in the history of this world had had it so good as us? (*VT* 42-43)

Timothy's contempt for human relationships (not knowing that Conrad Dehmel is the husband of "the only human being [he] ever really cared for" [*VT* 305]) and historical truth (accusing Dehmel of Gestapo atrocities which he was really trying to prevent) leads to the murder of an innocent man. Archetypally, the renegade son kills the husband of his surrogate mother.

John Wellfleet, whose story is a brief non-dramatic frame and half-time interlude, is heir to his relatives' memoirs. In contrast to both, he is a passive observer who enjoyed the permissive sex-and-drug culture (*VT* 26) and suffered the repressive backlash (*VT* 115). He draws together all the parallels of these allegorical characters, ostensibly to offer wisdom to André Gervais, but really to give didactic exempla to our era of the perils of extreme patrism and matrism, and the virtues of political and social conservatism.

Voices in Time, despite its ambitious scope and its technical complexities, is not wholly successful. As most critics have noted, it displays MacLennan's characteristic strengths and weaknesses in an historical perspective that intensifies both. Conrad Dehmel's story is a moving, dramatic narrative, and his character is sympathetic and convincing. Timothy, however, is a cliché-spouting stereotype who reveals which side of the generation gap his creator is on. And John is no George Stewart; his character and life are both unrealized sketches. The plot of the novel is complicated and often suspenseful (in the Germany sections) but too many coincidences (especially surrounding Conrad's death) weaken its impact.

The strongest criticism, however, concerns the novel's evangelistic didacticism. Apocalyptic horrors and the destruction of civilization too often produce an hysterical tone and reactionary rant in the elderly narrator/authorial spokesman (for example, *VT* 242). This is admittedly a thesis novel, and many of its insights on twentieth-century civilization reflect a thoughtful, consistent conservatism, a respectable ideological stance as critics from both the right and left have agreed. However, the pop psychology (Freud on Hitler and the sixties) and superficial sociology (the similarities between Nazis and *separatistes*) can become strained and unconvincing. More seriously, some of the stereotyping, especially of Jews (for example, Hanna Erlich and Esther Stahr [*VT* 47, 64]) is "very dangerous nonsense." Roger Hyman points out that, "It is darkly ironic that the author of a book dealing with the Nazis should so blatantly caricature the people they tried to destroy. . . . Indeed, it is precisely this mystification of the Jews which leads to the kind of antisemitic propaganda MacLennan would be the first to abhor" (321-22).

Though one might question the depth of MacLennan's psychological and sociopolitical analysis, once again his religious themes display a sophisticated awareness of developments in modern theology in order to confront the massive evil of the twentieth century and offer a tentative optimism for the human race. Even critics who have tended to criticize his "ideological bias that resolutely refuses to see the brutalities present in capitalism" have praised the "enormous importance" of his question: "Has the modern world so bereft itself of personal and public values that it is doomed to disintegration?" This "fundamental [question] of the century . . . lifts the book out of national place and makes it a significant novel in Western culture" (Mathews, "Night" 5-6). But the problem, again, is that the novel is "thematically weighty" but "sometimes not persuasive" to the reader (Hoy, "MacLennan" 194). MacLennan's theological themes are profound but not translatable into fiction; his portrayal of God's grace in nature functions as dogma not drama because of the abstract, subjective, vaguely pantheistic and mystical qualities of his "God of Evolution":

> The God I believe in is not the God of my Calvinist ancestors, though some of Him was present in that God, also. He is not the God of the ancient Jews, though even more of Him was present there. He is the God who manifests Himself in evolution, in all living creatures, and He moves in just as mysterious a way His wonders to perform as He did when the psalmist looked up to the hills and hoped for the best. (qtd. in E. Cameron, *Life* 348)

During the decade he was writing *Voices in Time*, MacLennan attempted further to define the God of *The Watch That Ends the Night* ("something larger than ourselves . . . the pattern of our lives and fates" [*WE* 372]) and of *Return of the Sphinx* ("this loveliness that nobody could understand or possess" [*RS* 303]). In 1961 he had spoken of a new generation, unfettered by the shame of Calvinism, who believed they were "organic parts in the great chain of Being," forging "a new sense of relationship with the Mystery our ancestors called God" (*Rivers* 11-12). Now he hypothesized that our minds might be immanent in the divine, "a pulse in the Eternal Mind" (*OS* 286), of a God who is "a form of energy built into the evolutionary system" (Twigg 95).

This existential-mystical-pantheistic theology which forms the thematic basis of *Voices in Time* is similar to Henri Bergson's Creative Evolution as interpreted by Paul Tillich. MacLennan's use of the term "*l'élan vital*" suggests at least a popular literary understanding of Bergson's theories (qtd. in *OS* 15). MacLennan shared both Bergson's concept of the primacy of intuition over intellectualism (cf. "Reflections" 31) and his interest in heroes and prophets in whom the "life force" finds its fullest development (for example, Catherine and Jerome Martell).

However, as the theologian Thomas G. Bandy has pointed out, "Bergson's conception of the *élan vital* . . . does not carry any specific religious meaning or moral demand" (7), and it is this deficiency Paul Tillich remedied in his "selective . . . appreciation" of Bergson's theories (4). Tillich agreed with Bergson's revolt "against the rising technology that devalued the human spirit and left existence meaningless" and his "anti-rationalistic,"

"intuitive," "creative," "dynamic" metaphysic of "the self affirmation of self"
(4-5). Tillich's major interest in Bergson concerned this doctrine of "the
mystical union of the self with Being-Itself . . . the ground of being" (6). He
connected Bergson's "concepts of process and becoming" with his own
theories of "being and nonbeing," "existential anxiety," "moral evil," and "the
demonic" (8):

> These philosophical ways of using the concept of non-being can be viewed
> against the background of the religious experience of the transitoriness of
> everything created and the power of the "demonic" in the human soul and
> history. (*Courage* 42)

Tillich appreciated Bergson's theme of "dynamic vitality" which counters
"existential guilt and fallenness" (Bandy 8). But his sense of "historical
purpose and destiny" (like MacLennan's) is stronger than Bergson's, which
denies the concept of transcendence: "In other words, so long as God is
incorporated into organism in such a way as to deny the status of the
Unconditioned, God is no longer able to mediate a sense of purpose or destiny
through participation in finitude" (Bandy 15).

My purpose is not to prove that MacLennan was directly influenced
by Tillich's reading of Bergson but to point out the remarkable similarities
between Tillich's theological interpretation of Creative Evolution and
MacLennan's religious adaptation of current evolutionary theory. Although
his rhetorical presentation of this faith in his fiction may lack dramatic
conviction for many readers, the theories themselves reflect a sophisticated
attempt to meld theology and modern science into a new vision of God.
Unfortunately, that new vision tends to resist fictional form.

9. Conclusion: "codified theology"

We have traced the development of MacLennan's religious vision through his
fiction. Since MacLennan, despite his denials, was a didactic writer who
cheerfully sacrificed form to content, it should come as no surprise that his
strength lies in his vision and his weakness in his art. In both cases, they were
largely a product of his faith. His view of life was compassionate, wise and
comprehensive. Though his conservative ideology was not always politically
acceptable, he has been widely praised for his universal sociological and
psychological insights. But if, indeed, he was one of our strongest traditional
social novelists, it was first because his religious faith invested human life and
social actions with eternal significance; this is the lesson of all his novels.

MacLennan's religious perspective was a dominant part of that larger
worldview of history and sociology — particularly regarding the development
of the Canadian identity — that determines all of his novels. He often
repeated the D. H. Lawrence dictum: "the novel 'treats the point where the
soul meets history' " and he admired the evangelistic fervour of writers who

have "made the novel a mighty instrument for human understanding" (*OS* 270-71), feeling that he too must offer his solutions to the spiritual dilemmas of our world.   Since he believed that "in any novel, content should be more essential than form," (D. Cameron, "MacLennan" 140), there is always the danger in MacLennan's art that his faith will distort his fiction. Since his religious concerns predisposed him toward thesis novels, his greatest weakness was the tendency to manipulate plot and character development toward a theological solution.   Therefore, his structures often appear schematically contrived: the endings do not grow naturally out of character or action but are conceived thematically and invoked externally. His major characters are inevitably vehicles for his ideas and spokespeople for his rhetorical interludes.

His strengths, however, are many and they are also partly a product of his religious vision. He is not a "post-modern"; his view of life is neither negative nor absurd. He has a compassion for human suffering, a respect for human dignity, and a belief in the ultimate worth of human action within an eternal cosmology. These values are revealed in many virtues: his complex, realistic plots, his generally likeable major characters and the delicious satire of his minor caricatures, his powerful action narratives, and the loving detail of his settings.

If MacLennan is obviously more of an essayist than a stylist in his novels, this too is partly a result of his faith. For he scorned the modern technical experimenters who, he felt, all seem to denigrate life: the famous contemporary writers of America and Europe who have devoted "their immense technical abilities to the dissection of cowards, drunkards, weaklings, criminals, psychotics, imbeciles, deviates, and people whose sole common denominator seems to be a hatred of life and a terror of living" (*OS* 183). This was not MacLennan's vision. In an era of spiritual disintegration his artistic vocation was not so much to seek "to forge the uncreated conscience of his race as to reforge a conscience that has been fragmented" (*OS* 246).

This is an admirable, if unfashionable, theological enterprise. But can it be realized within the artistic form of the realistic novel, a form which is equally unfashionable in the context of post-modernism? For Charles Glicksberg, the realistic power of religious novelists such as Greene and Mauriac depends on the dramatization of religion "as experience, as spiritual conflict, as vision and aspiration, struggle and search and suffering, not as codified theology" (73). In the tradition of the great religious novelists, Hugh MacLennan also attempted to dramatize the spiritual conflicts of modern life and to portray a spiritual resolution which arises out of existential experience. That his fiction often tends to become "codified theology" is partly a result of his didactic, thesis-centred form. But it is largely a product of the idealistic and subjective theological model, based on liberal Protestantism, which he invoked as his faith, but which could not completely sustain his fiction.

III

MORLEY CALLAGHAN

1. Introduction

Although he did not share MacLennan's nationalistic vocation to define this country in fiction, Morley Callaghan was arguably the other most important founding father of the modern Canadian novel. One of Canada's most prolific writers for over sixty years, he produced in that time sixteen novels, five books of short stories and novellas, a book of memoirs, a couple of plays, and innumerable articles. He was also a major religious novelist, for the distinctive and personal view of life which characterized all of his writings was based on a religious view of humanity in God's world. In a time of rapidly changing social mores and perspectives, he portrayed the tension between the sacred and the secular in our modern world with fidelity both to the social context and to his religious vision. Callaghan always displayed an intuitive understanding of the complexities of the individual's existential struggle against "sin, the world, and the devil" and toward "grace" and personal salvation. In his attempt to commune intimately with what he called the "despairing questions" and the "secret loneliness" of modern life, "the dead of night in a man's heart," he used the vision and form of his art, for "in the glory of form is a sense of eternity" ("excerpt" 20-21). Callaghan presented humanity's spiritual struggles in secular analogies and the eternal solution, not in abstract dogma, but in drama with all the ambiguities and paradoxical mysteries of human life.

Callaghan's religious vision arose naturally out of his Roman Catholic background, but it was more instinctive than intellectual and more empirical than dogmatic. It was the vision of a world redeemed; at a historical point in time the sacred became incarnate in the secular and this Incarnation redeemed the temporal and gave it ultimate worth. It was this "view of life" that distinguished Callaghan as a "religious novelist." However, he denied that he wrote "thesis books," or that he deliberately sat down "to write religious books." And, while not quite "hopelessly corrupt theologically," he was not a consciously orthodox Roman Catholic (Weaver 23-25). In fact, like Graham

Greene and François Mauriac, he was a "Catholic who was a novelist, not a Catholic novelist" (Stratford 289). For he reserved the right of unorthodoxy for all "real writers":

> A real writer, that very rare thing — a man who looks at the world out of his own eyes and judges it according to the best part of himself, whatever truth he has in him; his loyalty is all to this humanity in himself. This loyalty can't be a deliberate thing, a self-conscious thing. It is simply his way of seeing things . . . ; all great writers by their very nature must be heretical. ("Solzhenitsyn" 72)

Callaghan did not, however, share Greene and Mauriac's particular heresies, what he called their Jansenist and Albigensian tendencies (Weaver 25-26). In *That Summer in Paris* he recalls how, as a young writer searching for a Christian aesthetic, he strongly rejected the dualistic viewpoint which he saw "running through modern letters and thought that man was alien in this universe" (*TSP* 148):

> My own problem was to relate a Christian enlightenment to some timeless process of becoming. A disgust with the flesh born of an alleged awareness of an approaching doomsday bored me, as did the flash of light that gave a man the arrogant assurance that he was the elect of God. (*TSP* 94-95)

Callaghan's own temperament, in contrast to this dualistic view, predisposed him to a "Mediterranean Catholic view of life" (Weaver 25). His natural inclinations were to live out his faith in the world:

> [I]t seemed to me it would be most agreeable to God if we tried to realize all our possibilities here on earth, and hope we would always be so interested, so willing to lose ourselves in the fullness of living, and so hopeful that we would never ask why we were on this earth. (*TSP* 111)

This religious attitude manifested itself in an artistic concern for and celebration of the temporal world in opposition to the fashionable modern authors who rejected "this world and the stuff of daily life" (*TSP* 229-30):

> Wandering around Paris I would find myself thinking of the way Matisse looked at the world around him and find myself growing enchanted. A pumpkin, a fence, a girl, a pineapple on a tablecloth — the thing seen freshly in a pattern that was a gay celebration of things as they were. Why couldn't all people have the eyes and the heart that would give them this happy acceptance of reality? The word made flesh. The terrible vanity of the artist who wanted the word without the flesh. (*TSP* 148)

Callaghan's rejection of this terrible gnostic vanity was based on the doctrine of the Incarnation, "the word made flesh," and it was this faith that gave rise to the distinctive marriage — and tension — of religious themes and realistic techniques in his fiction.

In *That Summer in Paris* Callaghan speaks of the "new dignity and spiritual adventure" that Christian artists were finding in the neo-Thomist philosophies of Jacques Maritain (*TSP* 94). We know that Callaghan was already interested in Maritain's *Art and Scholasticism* in 1929 (*TSP* 103), and in the winter of 1933 they became friends when the Catholic philosopher was teaching at the Institute for Medieval Studies at St. Michael's College (Callaghan's alma mater). This friendship lasted for many years, but 1933 marked an important turning point in Callaghan's writing.

It is impossible to attribute the religious themes in Callaghan's novels directly to Maritain's theology. Callaghan was proud of his long friendship with "the great Jacques Maritain," of Maritain's praise for *Such Is My Beloved*, and of his appreciation of *The Loved and the Lost* as "a great religious book." But Callaghan denied a direct adoption of Maritain's doctrines: "He and I had in common a belief in the essential dignity of the individual. That was the basis of our communion, and he knew it. Doctrinal matters were way outside" (Fetherling 14, 16). The novelist, while interested in metaphysics (*TSP* 103), seems to have assimilated ideas from his discussions with Maritain (J. O'Connor 147), rather than consciously to have turned philosophy into fiction.

In this practice, of course, he was in accord with Maritain's own precepts. Christian art is "the art of humanity redeemed" (Maritain, *Art* 68), but:

> [A]ny philosophical thesis imposed on a work of art tends to corrupt its transcendence. The presence of a particular idea in a work must be entirely natural, not consciously forced. For example, it would be impossible to create an expressly Christian work of art. For Maritain, Christian art can only result when a profoundly and sincerely Christian person creates a beautiful work in which he expresses himself. It is the work of an artist possessed by divine love. (Dunaway 106)

Nevertheless, in this theory of art, as in many other vital areas, there are striking parallels between Maritain's thought and Callaghan's themes, and the philosophy can often illuminate the fiction. *Integral Humanism* is Maritain's most important analysis of the application of religious principles to the secular realm, and it establishes the framework for Thomist responses to all particular temporal issues including those in *The Rights of Man and Natural Law*. *Integral Humanism* is the text of six lectures delivered in Santander in August 1934 — the same year as *Such Is My Beloved* was published and dedicated to the philosopher: "to those times with M. in the winter of 1933."

In *Integral Humanism* Maritain rejects inhuman totalitarian systems for a Christian humanism that "tends essentially to render man more truly human. . . . [I]t at once demands that man develop the virtualities contained within him, his creative forces and the life of reason, and work to make the forces of the physical world instruments of his freedom" (2). He characterizes pure anthropocentric humanism as a "metaphysic of *freedom without grace*" and Calvinist-Jansenist Christianity as a "theology of grace without freedom" (20). His solution is "that the creature be truly respected *in* its connection with God and *because* receiving everything from Him; humanism, but theocentric humanism, rooted where man has his roots, integral humanism, humanism of the Incarnation" (72).

Following this, man must achieve an *"evangelical consciousness-of-self"* (*Integral* 76): the knowledge of human sin and divine mercy, of human freedom and spiritual grace. This new man will establish the new Christendom, "a veritable socio-temporal realization of the Gospel," since ". . . it is in vain that one affirms the dignity and vocation of the human person if one does not work to transform conditions which oppress him, and to bring it about that he can eat his bread with dignity" (*Integral* 94). And the new Christendom demands "a new style of sanctity, which one can characterize above all as the sanctity and sanctification of *secular* life" (*Integral* 123). Although the temporal order is "a divided and ambiguous domain," the Gospel tells us that "the world is saved in hope, and the blood of Christ, the vivifying principle of the redemption, acts already within it," and there is no more segregation of the sacred and the secular. The Christian, therefore, must work for "*a* realization of the Gospel exigencies and of Christian practical wisdom in the socio-temporal order — a realization which is itself thwarted, in fact, and more or less marked and deformed by sin" (*Integral* 126). This new Christendom, which is communal, personalist, and peregrinal (*Integral* 133-36), will be a society "brought about on earth by the passing of something divine, namely, love, into human means and into human work itself" (*Integral* 203). This means that in art and in life "the temporal wants to be vivified by the spiritual":

> In reality, the justice of the gospel and the life of Christ within us want the whole of us, they want to take possession of everything, to impregnate all that which we are and all that which we do, in the secular as well as in the sacred. Action is an epiphany of being. (*Integral* 293)

From the beginning Callaghan's works were marked by this same strong humanistic compassion for the individual in his socio-historic condition and a moral concern for his freedom and dignity. However, in his first three novels he seems to have searched vainly for a theology that would vivify the secular with a glimpse of the sacred. In a conflict of current naturalistic theories with his own religious perspectives, his heroes struggle in vain to escape their environments, their pasts, and their own sins to find meaning, hope, freedom, and love — the intimations of grace in nature.

Influenced by the theories of Maritain — popular among liberal Catholic intellectuals at that time — Callaghan in the mid-1930s found a focus for his art in the doctrines of Christian humanism. The three novels from the middle of this decade are his most overtly religious, and many critics would say his best. They present a world struggling with sin but eternally redeemed, in which the dignity of humanity is rooted in the Incarnation. Human beings have free will to sin but also the responsibility to seek God's grace and forgiveness. And secular saints attempt to realize divine love in human relationships, thus bringing the Gospel into the socio-temporal realm. However, Callaghan was neither a philosopher nor a dogmatic theologian. He was a realistic novelist with an empirical awareness of the tension between the sacred and the secular in life and the very ambiguous ways in which grace operates in nature. Therefore, even in these three biblical parables there are few clear-cut victories for the Gospel or happy solutions for the characters.

In Callaghan's later novels his view of the existential struggle between nature and grace becomes increasingly complex, and there is a greater concentration on the secular realm as the only possible forum for any realization of the sacred. He expressed his personal feelings in an interview in 1971:

> Another interesting question is, how is anybody redeemed? . . . At the end of your life, the whole question should be, How did you manage to get along with people? If you say, Well, I lived my life in the desert, loving God, to my temperament that doesn't mean anything. Okay, kid, you dropped out, you're a saint in the desert, a hermit. Great, you like that kind of thing, but you know nothing about human beings. From my view you know nothing about love. And if you know nothing about human love, . . . you can't know anything about divine love. I hate the person who loves the idea. (D. Cameron, "Callaghan" 23)

This sentiment may be an inevitable development of Christian humanism when the emphasis shifts to human involvement away from a clear balance with Christian theology. This faith has resulted in Callaghan's fictional commitment to the realities of life and to the compassion for humanity that illuminate his books. But it has also been responsible for his central conceptual weakness. Desmond Pacey pointed this out many years ago and later novels have only confirmed it:

> Callaghan, though himself a Catholic, is a proponent of a liberal and humanitarian Christianity. The defect of that type of Christianity, and of much of Callaghan's work, is that it often loses sight of the reality of evil. One feels the lack, in Callaghan's novels and stories, of any definite standards by which his characters are to be judged. He succeeds admirably in revealing the shoddiness of most of the prevailing standards, but when it is a matter of suggesting alternatives he can offer only vague words like simplicity, tenderness and compassion. The result is that all of Callaghan's work has a certain moral flabbiness. . . . Of the novel, however, we demand

a firm philosophy, a clearly articulated sense of values, and instead of that Callaghan invites us merely to a feast of pity. (Pacey, *Creative* 211)

Having considered the development of Callaghan's theological themes, we can now see the effect that they have had on his fictional techniques. In *That Summer in Paris* Callaghan outlines his artistic creed of realism, according to the fashion of the twenties and the influences of Sherwood Anderson and Ernest Hemingway:

> It was this: strip the language, and make the style, the method, all the psychological ramifications, the ambience of the relationships, all the one thing, so the reader couldn't make separations. Cezanne's apples. The appleness of apples. Yet just apples. (*TSP* 148)

However, Callaghan also viewed this aesthetic as a moral, religious commitment, not to orthodoxy ("fat comfortable inert people who agreed to pretend, agreed to accept the general fraud, the escape into metaphor") but to honesty ("Tell the truth cleanly") (*TSP* 20). The real artist must portray the "concrete reality" of life in words "as transparent as glass" (*TSP* 21) in a rejection of modern dualistic heresies ("the terrible vanity of the artist who wanted the word without the flesh" [*TSP* 148]). Never a post-modern, Callaghan throughout his career believed in the mimetic function of art and the transparency of language.

Moreover, despite his denunciation of metaphor, Callaghan's logocentric fictional form ("the word made flesh" [*TSP* 148]) implies a metaphysics of presence behind his simple realistic surfaces. "I was loyal to my search for the sacramental in the lives of people," he said in 1983, "to find the extraordinary in the ordinary that used to be considered the great and only aim of art" ("Interview" 17). In realizing this aim, however, he was never entirely successful. Whether the critics call them "parables" (Woodcock, "Eurydice") or "two worlds" (McPherson), his novels attempt to create a temporal universe with the transparent fidelity of realistic techniques and the inner illumination of religious themes. He is combining Chekhovian objectivity with Christian humanism when he says: "The great fiction-writer, then, must not only have a view of man as he is, but of man as he ought to be" ("Novelist" 32). Callaghan may have underestimated, however, the difficulties of integrating faith and fiction. F. W. Watt calls realism and religion "two opposite extremes" that must be married with great tact, and points out Callaghan's frequent lapses:

> Callaghan is the kind of novelist who tries to reach his goal by simultaneously working from two opposite extremes. Being a realist, he enjoys making acute observations and providing accurate notations of physical appearances, turns of conversation and thought, and behaviour. Being a religious writer, he is inspired by glimpses of patterns or significant forms which promise to make all nature meaningful. Ideally these two

processes meet: accurate notation coincides with meaning, and there is an explosion of light, a point of illumination. Where they do not meet, we get the wayward piling up of naturalistic detail empty of significance, or — and this is more often Callaghan's weakness — distortions or false notes in the realistic texture, stilted, factitious, unconvincing effects of dialogue or gesture. (Watt, "Letters 1961" 455)

As a Catholic writer with a sacramental view of nature redeemed and imbued with grace, Callaghan would not have agreed that reality and religion are antithetical. Nevertheless, Watt has articulated the problem for the religious writer of illuminating the holy in the daily. Callaghan's solution was different from MacLennan's and produced markedly different strengths and weaknesses in his fiction.

While, as I have suggested, MacLennan seems to have begun his novels with a thesis, Callaghan began his with a (male) character. He then allowed the character to determine the action; this is the decision for a "character-centred" novel that (as we saw in the Introduction) many of the best religious writers have taken in order to avoid the apparent manipulation of the plot by a religious thesis (MacLennan's chief weakness). Therefore, Callaghan believed his novels "end in terms of the people themselves rather than in terms of the pattern for that kind of material" (D. Cameron, "Callaghan" 25).

Callaghan also, like Greene and Mauriac, had a customary attitude of deep compassion for his characters and, as he said, an almost "anarchistic" sense of the "unyielding" integrity and autonomy of the individual (D. Cameron, "Callaghan" 29-30). No doubt these values were a product of his Christian "personalism" as was his attitude of "Christ-like identification" (Stratford 220) with sinful humanity and his characterization which increasingly stressed human free will and potential, and the individual's eternal worth and vocation in the light of the Incarnation (Maritain, *Integral* 133-36). For Callaghan, as for Greene, "Le pécheur est au coeur même de chrétienté. . . . Nul n'est aussi compétent que le pécheur en matière de chrétienté. Nul, si ce n'est le saint" (*Heart*, epigraph). In Callaghan's books the sinner and the saint are frequently confused. Yet, as we have seen, he did not share Greene's Jansenist preoccupation with the sins of the flesh (*TSP* 94-95). Much more than MacLennan, Callaghan portrays the seedy case-histories of life for which there are few conventionally happy endings. But his view, while realistic, is neither pathetic nor pessimistic; the muted spiritual optimism in his novels rests on his Christian humanism and his "Mediterranean Catholic" view of the grace operating, however ambiguously, in nature.

Callaghan's narrative point of view is limited or selective omniscience (now known as "free indirect discourse" [New 164]), a voice particularly consistent with his compassionate identification with his characters. He most often focuses on one narrative centre, usually the protagonist, confining himself to the language rhythms and intellectual awareness of the character, moving between internal and external vantage points as necessary. In this way he attempts to delve into the souls of his characters and dramatize their spiritual struggles with compassionate empathy, without surrendering his own vision of the unity and purpose of life.

This brings us again, however, though by a different route, to Callaghan's chief weakness. And, as we saw in the Introduction, it is an occupational hazard for religious writers, such as Greene and Mauriac, who employ techniques similar to Callaghan's. His compassionate attitude, his undiscriminating generosity of characterization, his deep involvement in the limit-situations of his characters, and the structural freedom he allows them without the tyranny of plot or theme — all these result in the lack of a definite vision or judgement conveyed to his readers, and therefore the impression of "moral flabbiness" (Pacey, *Creative* 211). This is the opposite of the principle defect in MacLennan's works. However, unlike MacLennan, Callaghan was not an academic intellectual, a philosopher or essayist. He was a popular columnist and radio-television personality. After dramatizing the existential questions of life so faithfully, he either did not wish, or did not know how, to resolve them. In positive terms, he refused to impose absolute metaphysical solutions on the ambiguities of life. In negative terms, the ambiguities become simply confusions.

As D. J. Dooley points out, there is a modern critical debate about the necessity for moral clarity in the novel. He cites the quarrel between Wayne Booth "who maintains that the novelist must provide a judgement upon his materials and accuses many moderns of ethical unreliability for not doing so" and Alan Friedman, for whom "leaving things in a state of irresolvable suspension may be the most honest thing for a novelist to do." I would agree with Dooley that both positions have validity in the broad range of modern literature: "It may be proper for a novelist to conclude upon a note of moral ambiguity, but on the other hand . . . sometimes his doing so may be an evasion of his responsibility" (Dooley, *Moral* x-xi). In his interpretation of Callaghan, Gary Boire would apparently take Friedman's position. He praises Callaghan's fiction as a "heuristic device" used "to illustrate a moral puzzle which is left deliberately for the reader to solve" (Boire 99).

However, while never as didactic as MacLennan, and increasingly ambiguous in his moral framework and unorthodox in his theological content, Callaghan throughout his career constructed novels that appeal to logocentric concepts of "truth," "reality," and "the law of love." In fact, the author usually invokes both rhetorical and narrative closure at the end of his novels. These obviously moralistic and religious novels arouse readerly expectations of moral and religious clarity which Callaghan fails to satisfy. I argue that the essential pattern in the development of Callaghan's novels is the dilemma of dramatizing Christian humanism — the divine in the human, the sacred in the secular. His most successful novels are powerful syntheses of faith and fiction, but ultimately the increasing difficulties of uniting the Word and the flesh create moral puzzles that are less heuristic than simply puzzling.

At the time they appeared in Canada, Callaghan's first three novels were distinctive and courageous experiments in urban realism. He seems to have been influenced by the contemporary literary theories of naturalism which offered a sympathetic explanation for the sufferings of humanity with which he compassionately identified. At the same time he does not deny the religious perspective that people have free will and responsibility for both their sin and their salvation. This dual vision leads to an unresolved tension in these novels between nature and grace, reflected in contradictions of both themes and techniques.

2. Naturalistic novels: *Strange Fugitive, It's Never Over, A Broken Journey*

Strange Fugitive (1928), despite its fresh realistic style, has evoked the strongest criticism for its lack of focus:

> Callaghan seems to have been feeling his way in this novel, and he put into it practically every element fashionable in the advanced literature of the day. He does not seem to have made up his mind whether Harry is a victim of heredity, of unemployment, of a vicious environment, of Fate, or of plain bad luck. (Pacey, *Creative* 212)

Callaghan treats Harry Trotter, the primitive, unimaginative, inarticulate hero of this novel, with humanistic respect and seriousness. He shows us that Harry is seeking freedom and dignity in his life and relationships, what he can only define as a sense of self-importance (*SF* 6). We see that Harry easily confuses this existential quest with the worldly dividends of "strength and influence and money" (*SF* 130), and the route becomes violence and crime. After being fired from his job for fighting, Harry leaves his wife because she represents a conventional bondage and resistance to his ambition. Impetuously stealing a truckload of liquor, he launches into the bootlegging business. However, his "foolish dream of power" (*SF* 131) only imprisons him in an underworld of escalating violence and unsatisfying sex. Finally he is gunned down in the street as a retribution for the cold-blooded murder of a rival hoodlum.

The novel is garnished with fashionable symbols, both Marxist ("the Labour Temple, opposite the Cathedral" [*SF* 141]) and Freudian (the fourteen foot phallic pillar Harry erects on the grave of his mother, with whom he slept until he was nine years old [*SF* 101]). However, the naturalistic suggestions that Oedipal influences and environmental pressures have contributed to Harry's downfall seem unconvincing and ironic:

Vera agreed that his life had probably been mis-shaped by childhood experiences, and in the evenings, when there was nothing to say and he was sulky, she led him on to talk about himself. He saw that it was a good story and told it to Jimmie Nash, elaborating on some of the details (*SF* 58)

At times Harry enjoys this psychological rationalization. But it seems clear that, however ill-motivated and unreflective the choices of this impetuous man are, they are still free and deliberate, and he is "fairly happy, going along his own way" (*SF* 131). Ultimately, he is just not convincing as the victim of a deterministic universe, "a world where there was smallpox and crime and little girls who never had a chance" (*SF* 20). Harry is responsible for the wages of his own selfish, greedy sin. Despite attempts to stifle his conscience and rationalize his crimes ("'I had nothing against the guy,' he thought. 'Only it had to be done'" [*SF* 202]), he is haunted by vague feelings of guilt, loneliness, and loss of identity and purpose: "He had lost all identity, nothing he did was of any consequence" (*SF* 140). Neither monuments to materialism nor orgies of self-indulgence can assuage this spiritual death, and his physical death is symbolically inevitable.

The problem with this reading is that it suggests a moral focus in the novel that is not clearly there. Callaghan's point of view employs Harry as the centre of intelligence, which in this case is a misnomer. We receive all our ideas and information filtered through Harry's shallow sensibilities. We may feel that this novel (whether as naturalistic experiment or moral exemplum) needs to transcend its limited, unappealing protagonist through the structure of a larger ironic vision. Unfortunately, Callaghan's compassionate identification with the character, which encourages us toward sympathy rather than judgement, also makes any ironic distance or moral standards in the novel as hypothetical as a naturalistic interpretation.

It is true that Callaghan offers some religious symbols as a counterweight to Harry's worldly aspirations. However, since these too are perceived through Harry, the intimations of grace in nature are vague and subjective, and witness rather to a lack of spiritual vision. Harry only dimly appreciates the significance of the cathedral. We are told that "you can't get away from it. It's right in the centre of things" (*SF* 73), but it by no means has that force in the novel. Harry associates its bells, which withstand fire and flood, with his wife Vera (*SF* 141), and it is suggested that she (whose name means "truth") represents his spiritual home and mother. He seeks her on Christmas Eve, and again just before his death, for a symbolic absolution and forgiveness of his sins: "I simply got to make things right with you" (*SF* 257). But her only real attribute as an agent of spiritual salvation is her sentimental inclination toward Catholicism (*SF* 50). Therefore, she is no more convincing as a spiritual alternative to the sordid secular values than "Grace" who was "simply a beautiful thought" for Harry (*SF* 160), and whose name is perverted in his promiscuous mistress, Anna (Hebrew for "grace").

The realism of this novel has been justly praised. The rapid, colloquial style, the precise vivid descriptions that illuminate the insignificant moment, the consistency of diction, viewpoint, and characterization in free indirect discourse (or *style indirect libre* as MacLulich analysed it [178]), all convey the gritty world of Callaghan's themes. And yet, Callaghan ultimately fails to fuse artistic form and vision, to inform surface detail with significant design.

It's Never Over (1930) presents a further development of the tension between naturalistic forces and the religious themes of guilt and grace. The consequent thematic ambiguity is such that two entirely different readings of the novel are possible. The title of the novel would seem to suggest a naturalistic theme. John Hughes is a much more articulate, intellectual hero than Harry Trotter. Yet, ironically, he is a more believable victim, caught in the web of circumstances following the execution of his friend Fred Thompson, as we see him lose his apartment, his job, his fiancée, and, almost, his life.

However, I do not think this novel paints a mechanically deterministic universe either. The sufferings that are "never over" are the result of human pride and selfishness. Fred Thompson, in accidentally murdering a policeman, may have been conditioned to kill by his tragic role in the Great War, but he had always been "violent, quick-tempered and impulsive" (*NO* 88). His sister Isabelle may have suffered social and psychological injustices after her brother's death, but her actions in the novel are motivated by an obsession with moral and spiritual suicide. Her priest, Father Mason, says "Isabelle has thought all the time about the sin. There's the complete moral prostration. . . . You know she'll go on trying to lose her immortal soul. I think she wants to" (*NO* 146). Moreover, she indulges a selfish, vengeful desire to enmesh others in her sufferings, "as if she had to plunge into the mud and drag everybody with her" (*NO* 91).

John, also, is not the totally innocent victim of "powerful naturalistic forces," "ensnared in a web of experiences which are closely related with his environment," "helpless to cope with [Isabelle's] destructive power," as Brandon Conron describes him (Conron, *Callaghan* 61-62). The casual mention that John broke off his relationship with Isabelle "after Fred was arrested" ("It was better for both of us" [*NO* 11]) becomes increasingly significant through the novel as she clings to him, and he more strongly repudiates her love and grief. From the beginning at Fred's funeral, he prefers not "to have a part in the sorrow and all the consequences of the death": "[I]t occurred to him that it was better to be up there in the gallery, sympathetically standing apart and not drawn into it, than down at the altar with Isabelle and her mother and Lillian" (*NO* 32). Although he is naturally repelled by

Isabelle's possessiveness, it is really the frustration of his own self-centred ego that results in his angry paranoia: "his own importance had been destroyed" (*NO* 209). When he forces himself on Lillian she accuses him:

> Oh, yes, you were the victim of your environment; wasn't it something like that? Nasty people of low reputation insisted upon being seen in your company. But you could go on hating, couldn't you, couldn't you. You did that best of all and had the strongest hates in the world till you were completely obsessed. (*NO* 177)

Not only does Callaghan seem, in my interpretation, to hold the individual responsible for sin and suffering, he also rejects the modern concept, demonstrated in both capitalist wars and communist propaganda, that "the lives of a few individuals are unimportant when the good of society is involved" (*NO* 195). The image of the crowd that gathered in sympathy with Fred and the picture of his haunted face recur throughout the novel, uniting humanity in a fraternal bond: "they're all crucified in their own way" (*NO* 137). It is John's sin that he symbolically rejects association with this suffering, sinful humanity.

More seriously, he is prepared to take a human life to re-establish his own feelings of self-importance. Proud, vengeful, "deceiving himself" that he is being objective and just, and desperately rationalizing his wounded ego (*NO* 200-2), John perversely distorts a priest's advice into a licence for murdering Isabelle:

> [H]is own importance had been destroyed. His own soul had been denied to him, but he had a plan that would restore his own feeling of decency and dignity. . . . He swung open the door, stepping out into the cold, exalted, excited, thinking of doing the act that would restore to him all the dignity and decency of the spirit, he, a man of talent, anxious for all the good things, was entitled to. (*NO* 209)

However, the priest has actually pointed out that "the dignity of the human spirit" can only be destroyed by one's own sin and guilt, and it can only be restored by repentance and grace (*NO* 207).

John finds a kind of grace at the end of this novel in a new humility and acceptance of "the bond" between himself and Isabelle that symbolically embraces all humanity: "[H]e was one with her and her brother and all of them, only now he was no longer anxious to get away from it; almost calmly, and with a new, unexpected humility, accepting it" (*NO* 217). He repents his former "selfish" isolation and denial of love, and finds a new contentment and a "new pattern" for his life (*NO* 218-19).

Throughout this novel, which begins and ends and is haunted with death, Mrs. Thompson represents the "calmness, hopefulness, and superiority over the circumstances of death" that the others strive for desperately in their self-centred natural prisons (*NO* 222). Her personal grace, it is clear, arises from an acceptance of life illuminated by a strong religious faith and a deep compassion for others. Her character is an ironic contrast to the hypocritical bourgeois Christianity of Dr. Ellwood and his congregation. However, her saving grace remains a minor motif, unable to illuminate much of Callaghan's suffering world.

As in *Strange Fugitive*, the naturalistic interpretation depends on an objective acceptance of the point of view offered by the hero, who is the principal centre of intelligence. Ironic distance and moral discrimination become even more difficult in this novel since John Hughes is articulate and persuasive in his self-defence. In the last three chapters, Callaghan seems obliged to offer an authorial corrective, which provides a subtle moral backdrop for John's final progression from self-deception to repentance and peace, through scattered omniscient comments ("deceiving himself," "a solitary man, apart from everybody") and symbolic correlatives (the baptismal cleansing of his daily swims). Nevertheless, the ample evidence for both naturalistic and religious interpretations of this novel demonstrates the ambiguity and irresolution of theme in it.

The religious symbol of the cathedral spire, seen in *Strange Fugitive*, recurs again in *It's Never Over* along with more prominent examples of Callaghan's "quasi-metaphorical use of imagery" (Woodcock, "Eurydice" 94), uniting realistic detail with symbolic meaning. The number three, the images of death and decay, and the face at the window are heavily recurrent motifs. They function effectively in establishing the claustrophobic atmosphere of the book, but, again, Callaghan resists giving these obviously significant details a coherent meaning. In *That Summer in Paris* Callaghan had repudiated the use of metaphor:

> Those lines, *A primrose by a river's brim a yellow primrose was to him, and it was nothing more*, often troubled me, aroused my anger. What the hell else did Wordsworth want it to be? An orange? A sunset? I would ask myself, Why does one thing have to remind you of something else? (*TSP* 19)

There is no doubt that the "primrose" means "something else" in Callaghan's use of imagery in this novel, but he has tried to preserve the realistic surface at the expense of thematic clarity by refusing to say exactly what "else."

A Broken Journey (1932) is Callaghan's most pessimistic novel; it is not "tragic" because we never sufficiently admire or sympathize with the protagonists. In this book Callaghan seems to be demonstrating the destructive insufficiency of both the naturalistic and the dualistic views of life. Both the morbid preoccupation with inheritance and environment, "the sins of the flesh," and its antithesis, the spiritual heresy arising from a "disgust with the flesh" (*TSP* 95), are shown to be unhealthy. There is a suggestion of the grace that will redeem nature and unite body and spirit, but it never becomes a fictional reality since his characters' journey toward it is broken.

The heroine's mother Teresa Gibbons is a lonely, disappointed, unhappily married woman who alternates between sensual indulgence and spiritual devotion: "There were some people who thought her an unusually devout woman, and some thought her an old hussy beyond redemption" (*BJ* 1). Her daughter Marion has attempted to renounce her mother's sins of the flesh for life in a religious order: "She had tried to live in a world far beyond her mother's sensualism, and had even gone to a convent to devote herself to the eternal Virgin that it might be a symbol for her life" (*BJ* 37). However, since she has no genuine religious vocation, she finds it impossible to repress completely her normal human passions, and she leaves the convent obsessed with the idea that she is corrupted by her "mother's nature" (*BJ* 41).

Marion's dreams of a honeymoon journey with Peter Gould to the Algoma Hills and "a clean, whitewashed room" at "the Mission" recall her cell at the convent (*BJ* 25), and represent another attempt to escape from "everything in the world" (*BJ* 14). Again she is frustrated; when her mother expresses her attraction for Peter, Marion perversely rejects him to avoid being drawn into her mother's life "by the looseness of her passion" (*BJ* 37). Callaghan explores the psychological effects on a sensitive girl of an obsession with naturalistic forces. Nevertheless, Marion's life seems determined less by heredity and environment than by her own weaknesses, rationalizations, and refusal to accept her human nature in order to realize her potentialities. Marion feels trapped in her nature and aspires to a grace that will redeem it. In fact, her allegedly corrupt body remains quite virginal until the end when her "fall" seems more indulgent than inevitable.

Her lover, Peter Gould, also sees the world in dualistic terms. Disappointed in his idealistic relationship with Marion, he throws himself too quickly into an implausible affair with the buxom, earthy Patricia in a kind of mortification of the flesh. As he explains to his brother Hubert:

> It would be better to start with a girl like Pat because it makes the renunciation of everything I wanted before more complete. You think my taste is pretty low. All right, it ought to be low to start with so I could work my way up to a new kind of dignity. (*BJ* 79)

The back injury that cripples his dreams, therefore, is seen less as the result of deterministic "Gods, women on stairs, and whole sets of circumstances," and more as the product of his own psychological confusion. He recognizes this when he says, "Anyway, if I'm crocked up, I got what was coming to me for messing around" (*BJ* 124).

The "journey north" for Peter, as for Marion, represents a spiritual ideal:

[H]e tried to ponder the meaning of its magic as though he were close to an explanation that could be grasped intuitively; only it was like staring till your eye ached at the brilliant white peak of a mountain that could not quite be seen. . . . He could no more do without wishing [for it], or feeling the hurt that went with wishing, than an early Christian in a period of dreadful spiritual dryness could do without longing for God. (*BJ* 93)

In the second half of the novel Marion, Peter, and Hubert reach their "new world" in the north (*BJ* 208). However, they have taken the prison of the self, "the small white room," with them from steamer (*BJ* 147) to hotel (*BJ* 200). And the escape from naturalism into dualism is magnified in the vast reaches of the Algoma Hills.

On the one hand, Nature in its inexorable physical grandeur threatens a dissolution of the individual's identity and "destruction of the character" (*BJ* 250). This is the aspect of the country that the Indian guide, Steve, embodies for Marion: "A woman really wouldn't be having an affair with Steve at all. She would be having an affair with this country" (*BJ* 225). On the other hand, this fear of naturalistic forces is constantly balanced by intimations of spiritual grace: "As the northern lights began to sweep vastly across the sky, she felt a strange harmony and peace all around her, and she felt herself groping toward it and trying to become a part of it" (*BJ* 208). Peter senses that their feelings of unimportance are really a spiritual idealism, "the soul" inside them "might go leaping up with a kind of ecstasy trying to get close to everything for the first time" (*BJ* 215). Hubert's answer to their existential anxiety ("we seem so puny and inconsequential") is the most positive: "Remember you're a piece of it, too," that is, part of "the godhead" (*BJ* 240-41). Throughout, their spiritual aspirations are ambiguously symbolized by the brilliant, white mountain "like an immense, crude, rugged cathedral of rock" which here replaces Callaghan's ubiquitous church spires in pointing the characters to God (*BJ* 230).

Of the three characters, Hubert is "the only one who has climbed his own mountain" (*BJ* 194). Peter resists both natural and spiritual forces with his thoughts of the city (*BJ* 237). And Marion jeers at Hubert's intimations of grace in nature: "There was clarity and unity and I was a part of the unity"; she mockingly calls it "a regular Pentecostal feast" (*BJ* 242). Marion's final surrender to Steve is foreshadowed in the story of the bronzed woman who sent her soul away before she was raped (*BJ* 54), and in Peter's relationship with Patricia. Marion justifies her sin as her inherited nature: "I'm no good" (*BJ* 260). But it is more plausible as a deliberate self-mortification and spiritual suicide: "I don't seem to have had any faith in anything" (*BJ* 263).

In the end Marion, who has vainly sought peace, love, integrity, faith, forgiveness — all the answers to an existential awareness of sin and suffering — prepares for yet another escape and quest and self-mortification: "She felt eager to go, eager to scourge herself by leaving so much behind" (*BJ* 267).

Behind her she leaves Peter and Hubert, still in their "small, white room" (*BJ* 270).

In this novel Callaghan demonstrates the inadequacy of both naturalistic determinism and dualistic idealism as answers to the dilemma of human suffering and sin. The problem, as in his earlier novels, is that he does not offer a consistent alternative by which we can judge the characters' responses to their predicament, and their final moral choices. The multiple centres of consciousness in this novel do allow for a more objective view of the characters' self-deceptions. The symbolism overwhelms the realistic texture at times but, especially in the second half of the novel when the plot slows to a crawl to accommodate the philosophical debates, the symbols do not provide thematic clarity because of their subjective ambiguity as products of the characters' hopes and fears. And since the characters and their motivations are never totally clear, the final impression is one "of human futility, to which the only reliable response is pity" (Pacey, "Fiction" 691).

With growing intensity in these first three novels, Callaghan portrays the spiritual element in life, and the religious values of free will, responsibility for sin, and a search for grace that will justify human existence. These religious themes are at odds with the naturalistic theories that are also given some credibility in the novels. In fact, at times Callaghan's treatment of deterministic forces becomes confused with the Christian doctrine of original sin: [Marion] muttered, "I'm no good, I'm no good, I'm no good. I'm no good. I'm no good, . . . I knew all along I wasn't any good. . . . You knew all along, too, God. . . . But I knew God, as well as You did, so You're not fooling me." (*BJ* 260). The tension between realistic and religious elements produces a complex view of the existential condition. However, it can also lead to inconsistencies of theme and form. At this point Callaghan seems uncertain about both the explanation and the solution for human suffering, but he portrays it with honesty and compassion.

Callaghan's treatment of Catholicism in the priesthood is generally unflattering in his early novels. For example, the central chapter in *A Broken Journey* is a short story (printed separately as "The Young Priest" in *Now That April's Here and Other Stories*) that portrays a young, vain, naive priest, Father Sullivan, as totally incapable of recognizing hypocrisy and dealing with sin: "He was still breathing irregularly and feeling that he had been close to something immensely ugly and evil that had nearly overwhelmed him" (*BJ* 145). In some respects this portrait foreshadows Father Dowling's character at the beginning of *Such Is My Beloved*. However, the difference in their characterizations begins with the fact that Father Dowling does not pass by the sinner on "the other side of the road" (*BJ* 90, like the priest in the parable of the good Samaritan, Luke 10:29-37). This is a measure of the change in Callaghan's perspective between the two novels.

3. Biblical parables: *Such Is My Beloved, They Shall Inherit the Earth, More Joy in Heaven*

Callaghan's three novels of the mid-thirties express his religious themes most explicitly. As I suggested in the introduction to this section, Callaghan was especially influenced in these years by the Christian humanist philosophy of Jacques Maritain. This theology provided a context within which Callaghan could clarify the tension between nature and grace in his novels, and a coherent perspective on life which was neither naturalistic nor dualistic. However, his artistic commitment to realism demanded that he honestly portray the inevitable conflict between the sacred and the secular, and the ambiguous results of any attempt to realize "the Gospel exigencies" in this "socio-temporal order" (*Integral* 126). Therefore, these novels are written in the form of biblical parables which operate simultaneously on the levels of realistic fiction and religious belief. In two of the novels, the endings suggest resolutions on the spiritual level which stand in somewhat uneasy opposition to the existential tragedies, but I would at least defend Callaghan's fidelity in these novels to both his faith and his fiction. Although he does not convincingly resolve the conflict between them, he surveys the battleground with more clarity and conviction than at any other time in his career.

Such Is My Beloved (1934) most clearly illustrates the striking similarities between Callaghan's themes at this time and Jacques Maritain's philosophy:

> [S]ociety is essentially destined, by reason of the earthly end itself which specifies it, to the development of those environmental conditions which will so raise men in general to the level of material, intellectual, and moral life in accord with the good and peace of the whole, that each person will be positively aided in the progressive conquest of his full life as a person and of his spiritual freedom. (*Integral* 134)

Based on the premises of Christian humanism, this novel explores the relationship between man's free will and God's grace in the light of the saving power of "human love, divine love, and the love of man for God" (*SB* 72). Set in the slums of Toronto during the Depression, it witnesses to the difficulties and complexities of realizing "spiritual freedom" in the midst of socio-temporal despair. In order to indicate some of the parallels, I have made conjoint references to *Integral Humanism* with some of my quotations from the novel.[1]

Father Dowling, "the most eager young priest at the Cathedral" (*SB* 1), is Callaghan's archetypal Christian: in the world but not of it. Dowling preaches on "the inevitable separation between Christianity and the bourgeois world" (*SB* 1; *Integral* 79), and plans "the building of a society on Christian principles" (*SB* 4; *Integral* 126). At first he is totally naive concerning the socio-economic realities which oppress his parishioners and

deny them dignity, autonomy, and their spiritual vocation.   But he is,
ironically, educated in both economics and Thomist theology by two
prostitutes who have tried to solicit him on the street:

> There was much he had not understood, there was a whole economic
> background behind the wretched lives of these girls.   They were not
> detached from the life around them.   They had free will only when they
> were free.   He remembered suddenly . . . how he had learned in the
> seminary that St. Thomas Aquinas has said we have not free will when
> we are completely dominated by passion.   Hunger was an appetite that
> had to be satisfied and if it was not satisfied it became a strong passion
> that swept aside all free will and rational judgement.   If he properly
> understood the lives of these girls, he thought, he might realize they
> were not free but strongly fettered and he would not be so sure of
> judging them. . . . [H]e decided that he must first try and help them to
> live decently. (*SB* 42; *Integral* 94 and 134)

Through his association with Midge and Ronnie, he becomes less complacent
and more compassionate for the complex temporal situation of his people:
"his love for Midge and Ronnie made much more comprehensive his
sympathy for all the wretched people he had ever known" (*SB* 248).   And he
confronts the hypocrisy and inadequacy of religious legalism and empty ritual
(*SB* 187).

        And yet, in the end, Father Dowling understands that the ultimate
answer to human sinfulness is theological, not purely "economic" ("the
perfectly organized state") or "sociological" ("sterilize the feeble-minded")
(*SB* 253-54).   His gifts of money have not reformed the prostitutes, as he well
knows, and economic security has not sanctified the Robisons.   Father
Dowling is flawed by spiritual pride and ambition (*SB* 34), and lack of
worldly sophistication and prudence (*SB* 176).   Callaghan is not painting a
plaster saint, as he admits:

> Well, Father Dowling is a human being and he's what we call a good human
> being.   And there is no doubt I'm hopelessly corrupt theologically — I am
> bored by pure innocence.   I don't know any pure innocents. . . . A man's
> nature is a very tangled web, shot through with gleams of heavenly light, no
> doubt, and the darkness of what we call evil forces. (Weaver 23)

His earthly mission to the prostitutes is a failure, but Callaghan appears to
valorize his spiritual efforts.   Certainly the alternatives offered by Father
Anglin (Catholic legalism), Bishop Foley (ecclesiastical hypocrisy), the
Robisons (bourgeois materialism), or even Charlie Stewart (Marxist
revolution) are not presented as positive values.   Despite his flaws, Father
Dowling represents the most perfect example of selfless love in the novel,
and, as Midge meditates on him for comfort in her jail cell, there is some

indication that he has touched the girls' lives with a glimpse of dignity and spiritual grace (*SB* 223-224).

In the end, of course, the girls remain social outcasts, and Father Dowling is crushed by the worldly corruption of the church he serves and obeys but which, ironically, "prostitutes [the] faith for the sake of expediency" (*SB* 264). We understand that his failure is partly a result of his own lack of "Christian practical wisdom," as Maritain put it:

> [T]he Christian must work for a proportionate realization . . . of the Gospel exigencies and of Christian practical wisdom in the socio-temporal order — a realization which is itself thwarted, in fact, and more or less masked and deformed by sin. (*Integral* 126)

However, he is also a casualty of the inevitable opposition of the natural world to the operations of grace: "the work of which I am speaking . . . is, according to the ordinary course of things, all the more combatted and all the more betrayed the more it succeeds in passing into existence" (*Integral* 126). And for this Callaghan has no comfortable answers.

As many critics have noted, this novel operates simultaneously on the levels of social realism and religious symbolism. Malcolm Ross has given a detailed analysis of "the structure of religious symbols" that informs and orders the "social content" of this book in his Introduction to the New Canadian Library edition. The ambiguity and difficulty of the ending are due to Callaghan's refusal to compromise his dramatization of the harsh realities of physical existence even in the light of a metaphysical purpose and hope. From a religious perspective, however, I think Callaghan intends us to see Father Dowling's sacrifice as a spiritual triumph, a fictional representation of the action of grace in nature. The symbolic structure supports this interpretation.

Throughout the novel, Father Dowling is associated with scriptural allusions to the Song of Songs and the later Christian exegesis of this secular love song as an allegory of the love of Christ, the Bridegroom, for His church. In his sermon on "human and divine love" (*SB* 78), his final quote echoes Callaghan's epigraph to the book: "Many waters cannot quench love, neither can the floods drown it; if a man would give all the substance of his house for love, it would utterly be contemned" (Song of Songs 8:7). His love "contemned" by the materialistic world, he becomes the embodiment of the title, which is a reference to both the Song of Songs (5:16) and the Baptism of Christ (Mark 1:11). Just before Easter, then, Father Dowling partakes of a last supper of bread and wine with the girls (*SB* 216). He is betrayed by Mr. Robison and sentenced to self-sacrifice by the bishop because of his Christ-like love and forgiveness of sinners: "a kind of divine love . . . a purely human love . . . they themselves were more important than the sinfulness they represented" (*SB* 262-63). After agonies of doubt and despair, he accepts the necessity of sacrifice "so that God could enter in in the mystery of transubstantiation" (*SB* 272), and he yields up his life and his sanity "as a sacrifice to God" for "the souls of those two poor girls" (*SB* 287). In this context he is explicitly identified with "the word made flesh" (*SB* 271), and his earthly love is itself a commentary on the divine, a contemporary "Song of Songs" (*SB* 288).   At last he experiences "joy" and "peace" and the benediction of "three stars" (*SB* 287-88) which symbolize the Holy Trinity or, more likely, the theological virtues, the greatest of which is love (I Cor. 13:13).

Nevertheless, this religious interpretation does not solve all the problems with the ending of this novel. The entire book has emphasized Father Dowling's struggle to redeem the secular world with the love of Christ. A solution that is valid only in the spiritual, symbolic realm, and apparently leaves the secular tragedy unresolved, cannot totally convince the reader, especially the non-Christian, of its existential and dramatic relevance. Part of this problem occurs because Callaghan again uses the protagonist as his primary, though not exclusive, centre of consciousness. We closely identify with Father Dowling and can perceive the ironic differences between his point of view and that of others who are more worldly and less attractive. However, the lack of a clear authorial distance and context makes the irony somewhat unstable and weakens the synthesis between faith and fiction.

They Shall Inherit the Earth (1935), in keeping with its title, manages more clearly to integrate a spiritual resolution with the existential dilemma and to dramatize it in secular terms. Michael Aikenhead, like "the prodigal" son (*TSE* 30), has left his father's home to assert his independence in the "practical," "scientific" world of civil engineering (*TSE* 10).   However, unemployed and bitter at the height of the Depression, he has lost faith in life and alienated himself from others in his sense of personal injustice:

> I know you think I'm suspicious about people. . . . I don't seem to have
> any faith and I can't recite a creed of any kind and don't go to any church
> and I seem to be pretty cynical. . . . I know I haven't many friends. . . . It's
> funny, but the more I worry about myself, the more I reject the whole
> world. (*TSE* 85-86)

His refusal to save his stepbrother from drowning at the family's summer home is symbolic of his self-centred hatred and rejection of humanity (Conron points out the parallels with the Cain and Abel story [*Callaghan* 88]). However, he will not accept "the misery and desolation of his guilt" (*TSE* 90), allowing his father to suffer for the crime instead.

Returning to the city, Michael attempts to escape his guilt and find a meaning for his life in the intellectual "faiths" of the thirties, but none of them can give him absolution. He cannot accept the Christian judgement on his sin: "free will and the responsibility of the individual soul, and the soul's destiny and all that crap." So, arguing from scientific determinism, he tries to rationalize his actions in a belligerent exchange with his Christian friend: "I just want to know if you believe there's usually a chain of causes going way back that shape the most trivial event" (*TSE* 113-14). In reply to this naturalistic excuse, Nathaniel offers little consolation to the "scientific point of view" (in a further development of Father Dowling's Thomist answer to the problem of sin):

> I never said anybody was ever absolutely free to make any kind of a choice. If the passion overwhelms you you can hardly be free. That's what St. Thomas Aquinas would say. . . . [But] You might be just free enough to have just a little influence on whatever happened. I think St. Thomas would say that. (*TSE* 116)

Michael then unsuccessfully tries to submerge his selfish individualism in the Marxist faith and find "order and dignity" for his life, and an economic expiation for his guilt, in a "disinterested hope for the poor of the world." Therefore, it is ironic, since he has been trying to rationalize the death of one individual, that Michael is shocked when his Marxist friend devalues the fate of another "individual," Anna Prychoda. William Johnson says: "She's an illustration of a larger issue and you can't stop to worry about her" (*TSE* 134-35). It is Michael's "deep concern" for her that finally breaks through his own self-pity in a "surge of love" (*TSE* 136). Therefore, even though it costs him the "infinite tolerance" (*TSE* 144) of the ruthless individualist, Huck Farr (whose name is an anagram for his treatment of women [*TSE* 127]), this love is the first step towards the freedom, dignity, and meaning he seeks (*TSE* 148-49). In this dialogue with the alternative religions of the age, Callaghan is echoing Jacques Maritain's theological rejection of scientific rationalism, Marxism, and bourgeois capitalism in favour of selfless, sacrificial love as the basis for human society.

Michael now longs to drown his autonomy and responsibility in Anna's "compassion and charity," "to lose his identity in love for her" (*TSE* 153). However, even this love cannot insulate him from the lack of "order" and "justice" in the world, "the meaningless strife of his life" and "the death and corruption around him" (*TSE* 194). He fears desperately for the fragility of their relationship. For, in his personal love, he is still as selfish as his sister Sheila: "It's like a little island for ourselves here and we can devote ourselves to each other," she says of her marriage (*TSE* 241).

In contrast to Sheila (and her "little private . . . boudoir world" [*TSE* 231]), her husband Ross, like Anna, is a saintly figure who "possess[es] his own soul" (*TSE* 20) and tries to save others. Like Mike, he has rejected his father's life, but in this case it is the "vigorous individualism" (*TSE* 84) which is really the ruthless capitalism that has caused the Depression (and perverted the "sacred" in humanity): "Jay . . . could not imagine a society among men where man did not stand alone, and where a man did not have a sacred right to demand that he be left alone to conduct his own business in his own way" (*TSE* 179). In opposition, Ross's "collective notion" is directed towards the "freedom and liberty" (*TSE* 84) of human beings in society which Maritain espouses as Christian humanism (*Integral* 134). Therefore, he has become a doctor, but he shares the same skepticism of Mike's scientific rationalism and materialism that Nathaniel has expressed: "Sometimes I can't help thinking that scientists don't know anything. They all work their own little gardens and they all hoe their own little patches. They specialize. They refuse even to consider the relation of one thing to another" (*TSE* 250). Instead of whining for social justice, as Michael does, Ross works for it in the lives of his patients: "He sees a lot of confusion and disorganization around him and thinks it's up to him to straighten it out" (*TSE* 240).

The wolf hunt that Michael and Ross go on is a "microcosm of life" parable which illustrates the conflict between their personal philosophies. In his "despair" and "fear" of the world as an existential jungle in which all men act like moral wolves, Michael is "really crying out against the meaningless confusion of whatever he had known of living, and his search for peace, and he wanted most of all, even without quite knowing how much he wanted it, to justify his preservation of his own bit of happiness and his own life" (*TSE* 248). Ross, "with peace and unity in his soul" (*TSE* 249) condemns the neurotic kind of love that is just "self-protection" (*TSE* 251). Confronting the slaughter of the deer, in "his coat of many colours" (like Joseph, proclaiming God's will), Ross expresses his faith for an existential world: "I believe that everything that happens would have just as much meaning, if we could only see it properly" (*TSE* 257). Michael cannot accept this, for he sees "no pattern and no unity and no justice." But, as he again demands personal justice, he senses that the answer lies in selfless love: "I know everything will have some meaning if I stop passing judgement on other people, and forget about myself, and let myself look at the world with whatever goodness there is in me" (*TSE* 259). Significantly, the stars that "shine impartially on the agitated and the turbulent and complaining living souls" (*TSE* 259), and the name that he clings to ("Anna" [*TSE* 253]) prefigure the ultimate solution to his quest — divine grace.

Meanwhile, Michael's father has been humiliated and impoverished by the suspicions cast on him by Michael's actions. Through his sufferings he learns love and humility, longing (like Ross and Anna) to lose himself in "communion" with others, "and, in losing himself, possess forever his own soul" (*TSE* 285). However, when the arrogant church people reject him (ironically after they have all repeated the Prayer of Humble Access that acknowledges their corporate sinfulness), his spirit begins to die in guilt and fear (*TSE* 288).

At the crisis of the novel, Michael confronts the death for which he has been responsible, and which now, by the laws of the personal "justice" he has been demanding, "would take Anna from him." With genuine contrition and humility he finally prays: "My God, have pity on me. I don't want justice. I want mercy. Have pity on me." And, having accepted God's will in "whatever there had been of life, and what there was to be of death," he is given the gift of new life in "Little Mike" (*TSE* 306-12).

Throughout the novel, all of the characters have been searching for various "faiths" to give their lives existential "meaning" (these motifs are constantly repeated). Michael now realizes the utter futility of all the social gospels of the thirties, sought as a panacea by those whose "souls were restless":

> They were all like himself, only some became Catholics and some became communists, and then it was too bad for Catholicism and too bad for communism, for such people as these in this generation only heaped the chaos in their own souls on whatever they touched. Such people were all like him in this, that they couldn't know peace or dignity or unity with anything till they were single and whole within themselves.(*TSE* 319-20)

Only in Anna's daily realization of the Gospel Beatitudes in secular life can he see hope for possessing both heaven and earth:

> She went on from day to day, living and loving and exposing the fullness and wholeness of herself to the life around her. If to be poor in spirit meant to be without false pride, to be humble enough to forget oneself, then she was poor in spirit, for she gave herself to everything that touched her, she let herself be, she lost herself in the fullness of the world, and in losing herself she found the world, and she possessed her own soul. People like her could have everything. They could inherit the earth. (*TSE* 320)

Confessing to Anna that he has murdered, according to the Gospel criteria (Matt. 5:21-22), Michael finally finds peace, grace, and absolution in her Christ-like "goodness," "pity and love" (*TSE* 324-25). Emphasizing mercy over Old Testament justice, she persuades the prodigal son to seek his father's forgiveness. In their recreation of the parable of the repentant sinner and the forgiving father lies Callaghan's rare happy ending.

The final section of *They Shall Inherit the Earth* demonstrates some striking thematic parallels to the Gospel of Matthew, Chapters 5 to 7 — appropriate since this Gospel emphasizes the realization of "the kingdom of God" on earth more than the other three (O'Connor points out that references to Matthew also occur frequently throughout Maritain's works [150]). It is from the Sermon on the Mount (Matt. 5:1-12) that Callaghan has taken the vision and values that are dramatized in the successful integration of the sacred and the secular in this novel. The themes, the meaning of the symbolic patterns (both religious and secular), the characterization, the objective point of view, and the author's moral stance are all much clearer in this second biblical book. However, in this resolution of the conflict between faith and fiction, Callaghan has had to compromise somewhat with the realistic novel. As is obvious from the quotations I have given, this is a novel of long philosophical discussions.   While both the setting and the characters' relationships are vividly real, the characters themselves are obvious representatives of various ideologies, and their dialogue and introspection are sometimes didactically artificial.   Moreover, there is some sense that the conclusion of the plot is not so much an inevitable product of the characters' actions as the resolution of a theological debate.   Still, this is Callaghan's most coherent "parable."

In *More Joy in Heaven* (1937) Callaghan returned to the tragic and ambiguous confrontation between grace and nature that we saw in *Such Is My Beloved*.   Is it possible, or even advisable, to work for a realization of Christian values in the socio-temporal world?   In examining this question, Callaghan again concentrates on the enigmatic figure of the saint, but here Father Dowling's prideful innocence has been magnified into the sinner-saint figure of Kip Caley. Callaghan has said:

> Well, I don't mean really that innocence is always crucified, but innocence is rather fascinating. . . . There's a very thin borderline between innocence and crime. . . . But you see the saint and the sinner, or the saint, let us say, and the man guilty of the sin of monstrous pride — there's a very thin line there because the saint in his own way has a kind of monstrous egotism. And the great criminal has a monstrous egotism. The saint puts himself against the world, opposes himself in what he stands for to the whole world — which he calls, of course, usually the work of Satan. But the great criminal also puts himself against the world and the laws of society. (Weaver 22)

This could be an "after and before" description of the reformed bankrobber hero, Kip Caley.

More Joy in Heaven was based on the true story of Red Ryan in 1935-36 (Conron, *Callaghan* 108) but is told as an ironic parable of the lost sheep returned to the modern social fold. Kip Caley is a repentant sinner who is reborn on Christmas Day and hailed as a secular Messiah. Within a few months, however, he is crucified by a howling mob, a victim of their exploitation, but also of the tragic pride that has corrupted his spiritual redemption with worldly ambitions.

Emerging from prison on Christmas, his "birthday" (*MJ* 22), Kip only wants to leave behind that self-seeking egotism that made him a criminal and a clown in society: "I guess I was always playing myself against the field, making my own rules. I never wanted to work with anybody — that's where I jumped the tracks. . . . I thought I was too big a guy" (*MJ* 20). He wants humbly to take up the ordinary, simple life of a "good man" (*MJ* 33). Again, as in *They Shall Inherit the Earth*, Callaghan uses secular terms to express Kip's "conversion," rather than the theological language of Father Dowling.

However, this seems to be Callaghan's testament against the naturalism expressed by the unctuous bishop of a hypocritical church: "Of course, as a Christian he [the bishop] had to believe it possible in a man to change the pattern of his life, but he knew it hardly ever happened. . . ." (*MJ* 52). Nevertheless, Kip has changed, and his redemption is specifically associated with the true spiritually of the Gospel parables of the prodigal son (Luke 15) and with an obvious pattern of Christ symbols.

The problem, and the irony, is that Kip is acclaimed as a secular redeemer by an anthropocentric humanistic society (cf. Maritain, *Integral* 28-30) that desperately wants to believe in people's ability to reform and save themselves; he represents "all the good resolutions" they have ever made (*MJ* 110). The philanthropist senator enjoys the "power and exultation" of playing God the creator (*MJ* 16); the mayor wants an evangelist for "his whole social program" (*MJ* 101); even the bishop uses Kip as an excuse for "feasting and celebrating for the prodigal son" since it helps him get his mortgage money (*MJ* 53). It is humanity's sinful pride and its use of others as objects that Callaghan is dramatizing in repeated images of burlesque clowns, cages, zoos, and the ice carnival where all the beautiful people in "bright masks" gape at Kip as if he were an animal (*MJ* 77). In this secular world, the perversion of "forgiveness" is a "vast tolerance" (*MJ* 60, cf. Huck Farr *TSE* 144), and the wealthy serve Mammon with a "thoughtless irresponsibility" (*MJ* 84).

Swayed by this "crazy, demoralizing kind of grandeur" (*MJ* 126), Kip now rejects the humble life:

> Listen, what would you have thought of the prodigal son if he had come home, and found his old man and his family had got a big feast ready and invited all the neighbours in and they were all getting ready for a swell time, and the son takes one look at them and refuses to sit down on account of them wanting to make a fuss over him? . . . A killjoy — too dumb and self-centred to see it didn't mean anything, unless he met them half way.(*MJ* 119)

But Father Butler warns him: "Maybe anybody who wanted an excuse to have a feast invited him out. . . . I wonder what happened to him after the feasting was over" (*MJ* 119). Kip begins to believe in his "apotheosis" (*MJ* 112) and to see himself as redeemer, advocate, and mediator, not between humanity and God, but between "the outcasts and the right-thinking people" (*MJ* 133-34). However, in his innocence he does not see that there is the same basic corruption in both levels of society.

Judge Ford is the chief representative of the "right-thinking people." He sees the facile errors in the mayor's behaviourist concept of humanity. In his sarcastic inversion of the title (and Luke 15:7) he points out the theological inadequacy of a naturalism that omits both sin and free will:

> No man is ever evil in his hierarchy. . . . There's no such thing as free will to men like him. Men to him are simply pushed around by forces working on them. They get a man like you in a penitentiary and train him and he expresses the beautiful godhead in him. Everybody is delighted. There's more joy on earth than there is in heaven. (*MJ* 154)

He, on the other hand, is so tied to his legalistic Old Testament view of justice and original sin, "the law and order he loved above everything" (*MJ* 121), that he too denies human beings both grace and free will. Therefore, Kip recognizes that the judge is just like the satanic criminal Foley (*MJ* 156), mocking Kip and tempting him to violence (*MJ* 107).

In growing disillusionment with society, Kip clings to the "faith in himself" that he sees reflected in the simple love and trust of Julie Evans and Father Butler (*MJ* 171). However, when he finally realizes that his redemption has been betrayed by his prestigious friends, and his resurrection corrupted into a sideshow by his own pride ("I've been clowning for months" [*MJ* 208]), he recants:

> He was thinking of the years in the prison, the nights when he had gone over and over his life, putting a new price on everything. . . . The thing he had thought so big, this faith, the peace he had found, the innocence he had sought, had made him a clown. (*MJ* 214)

In a personal Gethsemane he struggles against hatred, revenge, self-loathing, and spiritual death: "[the prodigal son] got pretty sore and saw that the big feeling he had was just a shot in the arm for the folks of the town, then he cleared out, hating everybody, and back he went to the happy hunting ground" (*MJ* 225). Nevertheless, he finally rejects the evil temptation represented by Foley (in a satanic inversion of the parable of the lost sheep [*MJ* 248]) and resolves his crisis of faith: "I found out that the thing I got hold of belongs to me — it doesn't depend on anyone else" (*MJ* 251-52). Ironically, Julie and Father Butler have already "betrayed" and "denied" him (*MJ* 249) as Peter did Christ.

In the final act of this tragedy, the Christian symbolism operates as a sardonic comment on the ways of the world. Kip is symbolically crucified between two thieves, trying to act as a "mediator" to "save" them from "evil" and "death," and destroyed by the "dreadful irresponsibility" of the society (*MJ* 261) that had so recently acclaimed him. He descends into a hell of hatred and despair (in the coal cellar): " 'Jesus Christ,' he sobbed. 'There's no place, no place in the world' " (*MJ* 263; cf. Luke 9:58: "Foxes have holes, and birds of the air have nests; but the Son of Man has nowhere to lay his head"). In the end, he ascends Julie's stairs to affirm love, freedom, and new life: "See — I wanted to tell you. . . . You brought me life" (*MJ* 273). In this epiphany Callaghan valorizes Maritain's key sentiment: "Every self-sacrifice, every gift of oneself involves, be it in the smallest way, a dying for the one we love. . . . nothing is more human and more divine than the gift of oneself" (*Reason* 196-97). In their "private peace" and love they are not allegorical Christ-figures so much as Christ-followers, flawed and human. However, their broken bodies and sacrificial blood are blessed, perhaps transubstantiated, by Father Butler. He, like Father Dowling, is "no plaster saint" (*MJ* 9) in his fight "against the field" of corrupt society (*MJ* 217), but he has taught Kip "that a man could violate the law in such a way his goodness would not be broken, but would be strengthened; charity came before law and order" (*MJ* 177).

For a symbolic three days Kip lies in a coma. When he dies, the Bishop, who ironically satisfies the worldly "pattern of law and order" rather than the spiritual priority of charity (I Cor. 13:13), orders him buried in unconsecrated ground. Nevertheless, Kip "had made his peace with Julie and the things he knew were good" (*MJ* 276-77).

At the end of this novel, even secular critics agree that Kip Caley's "personal salvation is achieved regardless of his society's complete misunderstanding and condemnation" of his "private faith" (Watt, "Thinker" 125). However, while there may be "more joy in heaven," Kip's earthly drama remains a martyrdom, compounded by tragic pride, that has led to violence and five deaths. David Dooley offers a technical explanation for the ambivalent endings of *Such Is My Beloved* and *More Joy in Heaven*:

> Both these parables show sincere and idealistic individuals in opposition to society, both invite clear and obvious interpretations, and both offer evidence to challenge or moderate these interpretations. The reason is easy to find: the figures in parables are usually simple and typical, the central characters of Callaghan are rather more complex. (Dooley, *Moral* 63)

Callaghan has resolved this secular story with fidelity to complex, realistic characterization and narrative, yet the final chapter is not tragic — it is ironic, though the irony is directed against society, rather than Kip. Callaghan's religious vision offers a possible transcendent consolation and transforming meaning to the existential nihilism, but only by thematic reference to a realm outside of that dramatized in his realistic novel.

Callaghan's three biblical parables of the thirties counter the secular religions of the era with a strong Christian humanism borrowed from Jacques Maritain. This faith illuminates the sacred within the secular lives of his characters and imbues their fallen nature with the grace of compassion and dignity. At this point Callaghan tends to resolve the inevitable conflicts between society and his saints with a degree of spiritual optimism which stands in somewhat uneasy tension with his earthly resolutions, both tragic and romantic. Nevertheless, in these, by most accounts his greatest novels, the dialectic of faith and fiction is best balanced, and the synthesis most profound.

4. Sinner-saints: *The Loved and the Lost, The Many Colored Coat, A Passion in Rome*

For the next ten years Callaghan went through "a period of spiritual dryness" (Weaver 20). He wrote articles and plays (including a dramatic version of *They Shall Inherit the Earth*), and travelled for the CBC programme *Citizen's Forum*. In 1948 there appeared his juvenile book, *Luke Baldwin's Vow*, and a fictionalized description of the University of Toronto, *The Varsity Story*, commissioned by the alumni. But it was not until 1951 that Callaghan reentered the mainstream of Canadian literature with *The Loved and the Lost*.

The three novels published from 1951 to 1961 demonstrate remarkable similarities, in themes and even titles, to Callaghan's gospel parallels of the thirties. However, the later trilogy represents a subtle shift in Callaghan's treatment of the tension between religious vision and the fictional world. That there is a constant tension in his work is reflected in the critics' agreement on "the terrifying ambiguity of the main characters, the final impenetrability of their motives and identity":

> The gods may know where Kip Caley finally stands between the extremes of relapsed thief and crucified Messiah or what lies behind the shifting features of Father Dowling — lover, madman, redeemer, egotist — or how to judge the "malignant innocence" of Peggy Sanderson, but we are not gods' spies or gods' sergeants. As I once remarked . . . "the special talent of Morley Callaghan is to tell us everything and yet keep us in the dark about what really matters. He makes us misjudge and rejudge and misjudge his characters over and over again; we end up no longer capable of judgement, but not yet capable of faith." (M. Wilson 81)

In Callaghan's parable form there exist two levels, and while the characters are judged and rejudged (and often destroyed) on the secular level, it sometimes requires a "leap of faith" for the reader to believe in the salvation which Callaghan posits for them on the spiritual level.

The form of Callaghan's later novels, however, has become more diffuse. George Woodcock says: "Abandoning the *récit*-like form of his best period, he has sought the complexity of the classic realistic novel" ("Eurydice" 99). This greater complexity and realism seem to be a reflection of his developing religious vision. After the spiritual quests of his earliest novels, and the balance (although often uneasy) between sacred and secular in his biblical parables, Callaghan increasingly concentrates in these later novels on the existential struggle for meaning, and he refuses to posit theological answers outside of that situation. The ambiguities of sainthood now are seen primarily as a reflection of the spiritual struggles within protagonists who come to realize that they are not saints. And Callaghan seems to be saying that a resolution to these conflicts must be valid in this world or not at all.

This is not, I think, a repudiation of Maritain's theories of Christian humanism, although, as I have suggested earlier, it may be an emphasis on the "humanism" at the expense of the "Christian" because Callaghan found it so difficult to resolve the tension between them in his novels of the thirties. In any case, his refocused concentration on complex fictional realism is in keeping with other religious novelists such as Greene and Mauriac who, after a period of explicitly "Catholic novels," turned back to expressing their Christian concerns in works without explicitly Catholic themes (Stratford 307). Callaghan may even have come to somewhat the same conclusion as Mauriac:

> The reason why most novelists have failed in their portrayal of saints may be due to the fact that they have drawn creatures who are sublime and angelic but not human, whereas their sole chance of success would have lain in concentrating on whatever sanctity allows to subsist of what is most miserably human in human nature. And this is the special realm of the novelist. (qtd. in Stratford 209)

The Loved and the Lost is one of Callaghan's most complex and difficult novels and Peggy Sanderson a most ambiguous "saint." Throughout the novel she is perceived through the centre of consciousness of Jim McAlpine, the hero. All the desires and doubts concerning sainthood, all the conflicts between nature and grace that we have seen in previous novels, are focused on her by him in his quest for the meaning of life. As Jacques Maritain wrote to Callaghan: "No, your book is not about the Negro problem, it is a great book about faith and the hidden workings of grace, and the ambiguous way of sainthood. . . . I love your Peggy" (qtd. in Conron, *Callaghan* 10).

Peggy is doubly enigmatic because, unlike Father Dowling and Kip Caley, she is not the novel's protagonist, and (with two exceptions) Callaghan never lets us see inside her mind. Her character is constantly, and contradictorily, defined by others — often as a projection of their own needs or fears. Callaghan, as we have seen, subscribes to the doctrine of original sin, and Peggy's character is, no doubt, "a very tangled web" (Weaver 23). Her "charming innocence" (*LL* 18) is coloured by defensive pride, imprudence, and even stubborn perversity, the "monstrous egotism" of the saint. The ambivalence in her character of the sinner-saint, and in the response she elicits, is symbolized by the union of the church and the leopard (*LL* 33): "gentle innocence" and "violence" (*LL* 101).

Peggy is characterized by her inclusive brotherly love, "the kind of relationship she wanted to have with all people, no matter what kind of sacrifice might be required of her" (*LL* 59). It is her extension of this love to the poor, black Johnson family that cuts across the white barriers and first alienates her father (a Methodist minister whose faith has been "corrupted" by his "respectable" materialistic congregations [*LL* 85]), and finally incurs the wrath of the Montreal Establishment.   Ironically, it is her lack of "discrimination," so "full of love" for "the great big happy Johnson family," that also angers the black community: "Guys white or coloured are wise to each other and don't have that much respect for each other." Peggy's "love" and "respect" for everyone are like a childhood innocence (*LL* 93-96).

Coupled with Peggy's inclusive love is a fiercely independent belief in her own spiritual "integrity" (*LL* 121) — the saint's "egotism." This "whirling-away feeling" (*LL* 83) is in inevitable opposition to the "rule book" (*LL* 94) of a society established on exclusive, racist, and materialistic barriers of self-protection and self-interest:

> [S]he, like [Saint] Joan, lived and acted by her own secret intuitions. Joan had shattered her world, and Peggy shattered people too. . . . She would shatter all the people who lived on the mountain and the people who prayed on the mountain. Joan had to die, . . . simply because she was what she was. (*LL* 131)

At the centre of this conflict is the protagonist and centre of consciousness, Jim McAlpine, whose vacillating views are primarily responsible for our ambiguous perception of Peggy. He projects the image of an "independent Man" (*LL* 2) with an "absolute faith in his own judgement" (*LL* 10) that, if necessary, can "say to hell with the job" (*LL* 28). Nevertheless, more than he admits, he is in bondage to his own ambitions (revealed in his childhood story of the Havelocks [*LL* 9]) to be "up there on the mountain among those who had prestige, power, and influence" (*LL* 52).

To this end he cultivates a relationship with his employer's daughter Catherine Carver, reasoning sensibly that "she fitted perfectly into his ambitious plans. More than that; with her own life she could carry him forward lightly and effortlessly in the direction he had mapped out for himself " (*LL* 106). However, as his friend Foley warns him, McAlpine has "the will to be ambitious" but he does not have "the temperament" (*LL* 71). And his temperament is irresistibly attracted to Peggy Sanderson. He identifies with her as an outsider too (*LL* 61); he idealizes her unworldliness as an "oasis of happiness" (*LL* 70). Most of all, his personal "discovery" of her sainthood gives him a personal "faith" and "illumination" (*LL* 59), reaffirms his belief in his own integrity and independent judgement (*LL* 115-16), and represents a rebellion against the "authority" he has aspired to emulate but subconsciously resented (*LL* 64-65).

However, the artist's instinct that makes McAlpine Peggy's defender also prompts him to play "Orpheus" rescuing "Eurydice" from "the dark underworld. Montreal's Plutonian shore" (*LL* 135): "You see something in the kid you think no one else sees. If you could paint it, it would be done and you could forget it. But you want to grab it for yourself" (*LL* 70). He fails to see that his "possessiveness" is like Catherine's (*LL* 74) and his paternalism like Carver's. His desire to remould Peggy to conform to their world is a denial of her integrity and of his supposed faith in her, and therefore justifies her "struggle" against him (*LL* 139): "In his scheming dream of breaking her resistance and remolding her, he failed to see that he was putting himself against her; that he was justifying her instinctive resistance" (*LL* 146).

The hockey game serves as a correlative and a foreshadowing for Peggy's situation. McAlpine comes to a full realization of Peggy's antithesis to the "pattern" and "rule book" of society, and he is shocked by the potential violence of all those (including the priest who represents the church) whom he includes in the forces "who stand for law and order" against her "uncontrolled tenderness and goodness" (*LL* 164-66). The ambiguous irony of the symbolic melee, however, is that the Ranger player is clearly and brutally guilty. Having established the analogy, McAlpine's defense of her is less convincing: "Aside from the rule book, that player was guilty, he thought. I'm sure Peggy's innocent. That's the difference" (*LL* 166).

Throughout the novel, Callaghan has presented Peggy, through McAlpine's confused quest, as a dangerous and ambiguous sinner-saint. Consequently, the reader may experience "a rhetorical situation of 'argumentative incompatibility'" (B. Cameron 75) when the author clearly attempts to valorize Peggy's faith and condemn McAlpine's faithlessness at the novel's crisis in a passage of authorial omniscience:

> His humiliating doubt was only part of the night's humiliation, he told himself; . . . With a compassionate understanding, she was letting him keep his belief in his good faith. . . . The loneliness in her steady eyes and the strange calmness revealed that she knew he had betrayed himself and her, and that at last she was left alone. (*LL* 202)

In the aftermath of Peggy's murder, McAlpine seeks "absolution" for his failure of love, but neither Catherine nor Detective Bouchard can give it to him. Bouchard's philosophic generalization, "What if we all did it? The human condition" (*LL* 230) is intended to implicate the reader, for, of course, we have been judging Peggy throughout the novel. It also forces Jim to admit his collaboration with society in denying his spiritual vision in order to ride "the white horse" of materialistic ambition: "When I knew I had her and could keep her, maybe I remembered that I too had come to Montreal to ride a white horse. Maybe that was why I was always trying to change her. That was the sin. I couldn't accept her as she was" (*LL* 232). Like Father Dowling and Kip Caley, Peggy is destroyed by the social forces of convention and materialism, "all the proud men on their white horses." As McAlpine recognizes his complicity and betrayal, he repents: "In a moment of jealous doubt his faith in her had weakened" (*LL* 233). But he is denied the transcendent vision that redeemed the protagonists of Callaghan's earlier parables; the little church, like Peggy, has "vanished off the earth. And now he was alone" (*LL* 233).

This is Callaghan's most "literary" novel up to this point. The "primrose" (*TSP* 19) has obviously become a great deal more by now, and the book abounds in obvious metaphors and symbols that beg allegorical interpretation: the church and leopard, the white horse and the black hedge, the hockey game and the little circus, the colours black and white, the snow, the Orpheus-Eurydice and St. Joan legends, and the central structural motif of the mountain and the river: "Those who wanted things to remain as they were liked the mountain. Those who wanted a change preferred the broad flowing river. But no one could forget either of them" (*LL* 1). Neither the symbols, however, nor the point of view (although the author often comments on and interprets Jim's thoughts) conveys a consistent pattern of meaning. Callaghan's final vindication of Peggy is rhetorically ambiguous for the reader (and the critics, for example, Watt, "Thinker" 126, Dooley, *Moral* 74, B. Cameron 75) because it is inconsistent with the narrative strategies of the novel. Peggy (like Father Dowling and Kip) may experience a spiritual apotheosis at the end, and her values may have a religious basis (as references to the little church and St. Joan suggest). However, there is little specifically Christian doctrine or biblical reference to give her "faith" (unlike Father Dowling's) or her death (unlike Kip Caley's) any metaphysical substance which would compensate for the secular tragedy. Like the little church, Peggy's faith, and therefore Jim's, rather than being embodied in the fiction, tends to vanish under scrutiny. However, in dramatizing the complexities of human life, and the struggle for spiritual meaning, Callaghan has — to his credit — so involved the readers in the existential situation, that their responses to Peggy are as strong, and contradictory, as those of his fictional characters.

In *The Many Colored Coat* (1960) Callaghan again examines the religious motifs of innocence and righteousness. Here, however, he clarifies the ambiguity of his themes, without losing the complexity, by specifically applying Christian principles to human relationships in this novel, as he did in the second novel of his previous trilogy. Harry Lane, unlike Father Dowling, Kip Caley, and Peggy Sanderson, but like Michael Aikenhead, is never portrayed as a saint except in his own mind. As in *They Shall Inherit the Earth*, the protagonist's spiritual struggles with the ambiguities of sainthood are resolved in the recognition that he is a sinner, and that his assumed righteousness is destructive to himself and to others. This self-awareness becomes his salvation.

Harry Lane is the archetypal successful man of the affluent, materialistic fifties. He is, ironically, introduced as a "good," "naive" man to whom "nothing evil could happen" (*MCC* 20). Although he is naturally honest and generous, his values are being insidiously corrupted by his job as a public relations man for Sweetman's Distillery: "Harry had always been honest in all his feelings about people. Now he felt he was developing a false relationship with the whole world" (*MCC* 24). Harry's "world of easy money" (*MCC* 37) also corrupts his shrewd banker friend Scotty Bowman, who exploits the naivety he sees in Harry to involve him in a fraud. Scotty says, "I think he's got a bad flaw. He's a kind of innocent guy" (*MCC* 35). When Scotty commits suicide, it is Harry who appears the villain.

At this point Harry discovers that his "whole life" and "his faith in his friendships and his actions" have been a charade. As Joseph with the coat of many colours was sold into slavery by his brothers, jealous at his naive sense of superiority, so Harry is now abandoned by all his friends. He becomes obsessed with the need for "truth" that will reaffirm his dignity and integrity, and "justice" that will publicly vindicate his "innocence" (*MCC* 168-69). These abstract concepts acquire the weight of symbols in this novel, as they did in *They Shall Inherit the Earth*, through constant debate and repetition. To draw attention to his self-righteousness, Harry becomes a "clown" victim in his coat, which is now stained and torn (*MCC* 183).

His antagonist in the novel is Scotty's friend, Mike Kon, the false "Witness" who has taken away Harry's good name and given him a torn coat. He is the public "Konscience" (*MCC* 174) whose testimony ultimately forces Harry to face the truth about his former life as "a job to con people" (*MCC* 180). However, in summoning Mike to a "court of conscience," Harry must finally examine his "own conscience" (*MCC* 112). The puns, of course, are also part of the manipulation of words as symbols. Both Mike and Harry are basically honest men, but it becomes clear that their "innocence" is corrupted by spiritual "pride" and paranoia, "vanity," and "egotism" (*MCC* 169). This dichotomy is reminiscent of Callaghan's earlier explorations of the ambiguous innocence of sainthood; the difference here is that these men spend most of this novel seeking, not to extend love to others, but to find self-righteous, self-centred vengeance: "The more you suffer from an injustice, the deeper the wound to your pride, is it not so? And then to correct an injustice you become like a raging lion doing violence to your own spirit and to others for the sake of the truth" (*MCC* 169).

In the exploration of Harry's obsessive innocence, Callaghan is also demonstrating the variability of "the truth about any man [which] is pretty hard to tell, because someone else always has another angle on him" (*MCC* 107), and the superficiality of the "public relations" that are necessary for his dignity, integrity, and "self-respect" in society (*MCC* 228). As Harry loses the support of public opinion, the respect of friends, and the security of conventional appearances, he begins to see the hypocrisy of society, "the whole world in false face," as Kip Caley did (*MCC* 230). Finally shedding the "old disguises" of "the old Harry Lane" (*MCC* 232-34), he realizes that God's truth (*MCC* 169) must lie in his own conscience.

Meanwhile, Mike Kon is coming to his own crisis of truth. Also obsessed with the quest for "justice," he is accused by both of the women who love Harry of a lack of "Christian charity" (*MCC* 253). He begins to have doubts about his judgement of Harry and, in a miraculous message from his father, Chris the Christian, is advised to "Judge not" (*MCC* 262). Mike tries to rationalize this:

> It's all right for God to say "Judge not." That's from where God sits . . . not you and me. . . . You couldn't live if you weren't using your head every day about people you meet and things you see happening. . . . I'm not God, Mrs. McManus. I have to do the best I can. (*MCC* 262-63)

Nevertheless, the sequel to this injunction, "that ye be not judged," ironically follows as Mike is summoned to trial for assaulting Harry. With the second courtroom scene the novel comes full circle. Again, as in *They Shall Inherit the Earth*, Callaghan suggests the inability of secular justice to arbitrate fully the relationships between human beings. After the judges and lawyers with their "courtroom justice" are finished, Mike the "honest man" confesses his sin — "I had no right to judge Harry Lane" — and finds "dignity" in his own "conscience." His gesture of mercy to Harry is "a gratuitous thing," like grace operating in nature, and signifies "a separate peace with himself" reminiscent of Kip Caley's (*MCC* 308-12).

In the original 1955 novella version of this story, "The Man with the Coat," Harry Lane dies of the injuries inflicted by Mike Kon. In the novel, however, Callaghan grants him a happy ending and his own separate peace with his conscience. Throughout the book, Harry (like Michael Aikenhead) has resisted all criticism of his "fierce and contemptuous innocence," any suggestion of his responsibility in Scotty's death, and all appeals to "mercy" rather than "justice" (*MCC* 288-89). However, on the eve of the final courtroom battle with Mike for "justice" and "truth" about his "innocence" (those words again! *MCC* 313), he realizes that he has been one of those "terrible men of old who walked in wounded righteousness demanding the vengeance of the Lord on those who had wounded them": "Then he wondered if innocence was like a two-edged sword without a handle, and if you gripped it and used it, it cut you so painfully you had to lash out blindly, seeking vengeance on someone for the bleeding" (*MCC* 313).

Finally, like Joseph receiving spiritual wisdom in his dreams, Harry forgives his persecutors. He confesses his universal sin of naive self-centredness and self-righteousness, and relinquishes his desire for revenge:

> The greatest of sins was unawareness, he had heard it said somewhere. A naive man! Was he offering himself to the court again as the naive man who was the old Harry Lane? Unawareness, by this sin fell the proudly innocent, he thought sardonically. Fell into what? My God it need not be

into corruption — why not into some awareness that could give width and depth to a man's whole life? (*MCC* 314)

Now Harry renounces "his old life" for "a new world of new relationships with people" (*MCC* 314-15). However, he realizes that his old love, Molly, will not be able to follow him into "the new world" where "truth" means self-knowledge, not the "justice" of her father's world of social respectability and puritanical legalism (*MCC* 316-17). It is the prostitute, Annie Laurie (her name, like Anna Prychoda's, suggesting "grace"), who has taught him that "mercy" is the best any sinner can hope for: "I was doing a little praying last night. . . . I just throw myself on the mercy of the court" (*MCC* 290).

In *The Many Colored Coat* Callaghan has embodied "an intuitive sense of the meaning of Christianity" without the "scaffolding of theology" (E. Wilson 113), as many critics have appreciatively commented. Most significantly, he has not resolved the spiritual conflicts of the protagonist in the metaphysical afterlife of eternal judgement (where presumably the ambiguous sainthoods of Father Dowling, Kip Caley, and Peggy Sanderson will be blessed), but has realized the gospel imperatives in the humanistic struggle of "ordinary people" who "looked as if they could handle their lives and be comfortable together" (*MCC* 318).

In 1958 Callaghan spent a month in Rome as a journalist covering the death of Pope Pius XII and the election of John XXIII. *A Passion in Rome* (1961) works another variation on his theme of the ambivalent sinner-saint within the symbolic context of the death and resurrection of the Vicar of Christ, and thereby demonstrates a further humanistic development of his treatment of faith in fiction. There are obvious parallels between the relationship of Sam Raymond and Anna Connel in this novel and that of Jim McAlpine and Peggy Sanderson in *The Loved and the Lost*. But the spiritual pattern is rather more like *Such Is My Beloved*: the hero attempts to redeem a fallen woman by demonstrating a faith in and love for the divine spark within her humanity, against a religious background of death and rebirth. However, although the theology is still Christian humanism, the emphasis is more strongly on the human element. Neither the protagonist nor his protégé is a saint, even at the end. Whereas Callaghan transposed, and consecrated, Father Dowling's secular conflicts and failures into the spiritual realm (an apotheosis he attempted less convincingly with Peggy Sanderson), in *A Passion in Rome* he translates Sam and Anna's spiritual struggles into secular terms and orchestrates their final triumph in the temporal world. Consequently, this secular analogy of the Christian doctrine of redemption and resurrection is Callaghan's most sensual celebration of the flesh and sexual love, as if to prove that he could not be accused of dualistic heresies and Jansenist perversions.

Sam Raymond, lonely, alienated from family and friends, convinced he is a failure in life and art, arrives in Rome ostensibly to photograph the death and rebirth of the papacy. But unconsciously he is on a quest for the meaning of life in the Eternal City: "some one place in the world where a man's life might take on meaning" (*PR* 10). In the Sistine Chapel he desperately seeks some "new conviction that at least there was still something left in the world to worship." However, in Michelangelo's "The Last Judgement," with its "wild, tormented nude figures, so fearful and full of longing and suffering from their sense of guilt," he merely finds confirmation of the distortion and emptiness of his life (*PR* 38-39). At this point, his fear and existential anxiety are symbolically linked with a world under the "hydrogen bomb": "The whole human race a failure" (*PR* 40). Sam refuses to accept Francesca's Christian platitude that "if we're all wiped out the human race returns to God," and he emphasizes the importance of humanity: "The great thing is to survive" (*PR* 40).

It is through Anna Connel (another "Anna" symbolizing the potential for grace in nature) that he discovers the theological worth of the individual, not in Michelangelo's portrait of sinfulness but in Maritain's incarnational humanism. Anna suffers from a more debilitating form of Sam's own existential loneliness, but he sees in her the divine "spark of her spirit" (*PR* 55). Recognizing that people should be more important than art, and transferring his frustrated creativity from canvas to life, he attempts to nurture Anna into his vision of her potential, symbolized by the sketch he does of her:

> He remembered how he had imagined Michelangelo passing her on the street. And how he himself had longed to do as much for her; no, more for her — something greater than Michelangelo could do on a canvas — transform her so she could have her own being and be free again in her life. (*PR* 183)

Though he has "no theology" (*PR* 79), Sam's view of Anna is rooted in the dignity of the human being as an eternal creature, "in the beginning, . . . ever now, and shall be" (*PR* 98). This is a precept of the "Christian humanist" as defined by Maritain, not by Anna's self-centred, self-pitying lover Alberto (*PR* 86).

Anna is a neurotic alcoholic, escaping from her failure in the "American religion" of success (*PR* 177) into a European fantasy. She attempts to find her identity in past mythology (as the Roman woman, Carla Caneli) and her self-worth in present sex. Her existential fear is also specifically representative of the "world's sea of fear," civilization living under the threat of "the bomb" (*PR* 142-43). And, for Sam, the answer to "the fear" and "the future of the human race" and "the whole question of human survival" (*PR* 205) is symbolized in Anna:

> In such moments she seemed to tell him of the wonderful resilience of the human spirit! The things she had endured — humiliation, brutality, despair — all drained through her spirit, all becoming, in spite of herself, summer ripeness. Out of misery and terror — the promise that the wisdom of smiling ripeness was all. Yes. In the happy glimpses she gave him of herself, he seemed to see how all the crushing experiences could be absorbed by the spirit, and refined into an awareness that the happy hunger for life was unquenchable. She gave him pride in life. (*PR* 195)

It is Sam's mission to help Anna realize her spiritual potentialities: self-"awareness" (*PR* 172), and a "Renaissance" "pride," not rooted in a false sense of either "innocence" or "guilt" (*PR* 194), but in "the wonderful resilience of the human spirit" (*PR* 195).

Anna's renaissance is symbolically associated with a larger Christian pattern. Her "pride" is humanistic, but it is rooted in her eternal vocation: Sam denies that we are all just "a bunch of tourists" on earth; Anna is "a singer" (*PR* 178). And her singing will be a spiritual triumph as Sam explains to the cynical Francesca: "I'm telling you, the Christian, about resurrection. . . . Out of the ruins of her life. That look that comes on her face. Something in her spirit survives. It's got to survive. It's the divine spark, Francesca" (*PR* 196). Moreover, the private spiritual and physical "passion" of Sam and Anna is juxtaposed to the larger background and central historic event of the novel. Anna is frequently identified with the Eternal City, a dead city "born again under the popes" (*PR* 231). During the illness and death of the old pope and the crisis of choosing a successor, Anna dies to her former life and finds, with Sam's loving guidance, a new freedom and dignity. She is, symbolically, "the widow" who awaits a "new bridegroom" and a "new life," as the Church awaits a new Vicar of Christ (*PR* 242, 254).

As Sam helps Anna free herself from bondage to sex, alcohol, and other people, including himself, she also gives him a new life (symbolically like "Lazarus" [*PR* 259]), a new faith in himself and the purpose of life. Throughout the novel he has been searching for a personal faith, and he experiences the longing most poignantly when the new "Holy Father" greets his people:

> He had no fixed beliefs. Making a virtue out of faith in things that could not be known had always puzzled him, and it seemed to him that all the doctrinal ideologies of his day had been fading into myth and literature. . . . He felt a fierce, fugitive longing for some kind of assurance that what men did to each other had some kind of meaning; a desperate hope that beyond the single judgements of men was some kind of sublime rightness of things to which everything happening could be related. (*PR* 334)

Anna has given him a glimpse of this "sublime rightness" in the resurrection of her spirit, but she wisely realizes that she cannot be his personal saviour, nor allow him to play "bridegroom" to her "widow" forever. She asks him for "faith" in her independent worth and in his own judgement.

After she leaves him, Sam is temporarily shattered by a spiritual "death" (*PR* 345). However, his "wonder" at her human "courage and self-reliance" overcomes his self-pity and reignites "the glow" and "pride" in his own spirit (*PR* 349). A prodigal son (like Michael Aikenhead), he decides to return home and make peace with his father who has been counterpointed throughout to "the Papa" (*PR* 247). Then he says he will: "[s]ee the ends of the earth and judge them. I'm on my own now. . . . And wherever I go now, I'll feel pretty good" (*PR* 350-51). Sam plans to revisit the Sistine Chapel and confront Michelangelo's Jansenist "judgement" of sinful man with his own "fiercely exultant" affirmation of the unquenchable spark of human nature (*PR* 352). Although Callaghan has made it clear, through the symbolic pattern of interrelated "passions," that the final resolution to this novel is ultimately and deeply religious (even "Mediterranean Catholic" [*PR* 336]), the terms of reference are most strongly secular and humanistic (the pattern for life he advocated in *That Summer in Paris* 111).

As so often in his novels, Callaghan again attempts a precarious balance between realistic plot and characterization and religious allegory, the inevitable tension between the demands of fiction and faith. As Milton Wilson puts it: "Callaghan's uneasy mixture of parable and case-history, of hagiology and sociology, has always threatened to fall apart, even in his best novels" (81). Still, I think this unresolved tension in his work has yielded the profound and paradoxical insights into human nature that distinguish Callaghan's art. This novel also has a virtue which is lacking in some of Callaghan's other books (for example, *The Loved and the Lost*) — a consistency of theme and point of view. The final hard-won humanistic moral, with its religious undercurrents, is coherent, believable, and unsentimental because of Sam Raymond's "hard-boiled, secularized, sardonic newspaperman's view that is maintained throughout" (Watt, "Letters 1961" 456).

Together with Callaghan's biblical parables, these three realistic novels are his most powerful evocations of the tension between the spiritual and the secular in our modern world. While his parables may demonstrate more theological clarity, Maritain would applaud his dramatic "engagement" (J. O'Connor 149) in the humanistic struggles of his characters in these mid-career novels. Together, these two trilogies represent the fulcrum of Callaghan's balance of faith and fiction — he never achieved such equilibrium again.

5. The law of love: *A Fine and Private Place, Close to the Sun Again*

After another surprising long hiatus, fourteen years this time, Callaghan's two full-length novels of the seventies show yet a further development in his treatment of the complexities of faith in fiction. At this point he seems to have moved farthest from the metaphysical realm of grace to concentrate on the struggle between light and darkness in the realm of human nature. These novels celebrate more strongly the irreducible mysteriousness of life and the ambiguous egotism of the sinner-saint that are Callaghan's trademarks. But there is a danger that, in a parody of himself, the complexities may have finally become merely confusions.

A Fine and Private Place (1975), written in the decade after Callaghan's aesthetic manifesto, *That Summer in Paris*, extends that memoir's self-reflexivity into the metafictional mode that characterizes his final period of writing and includes *A Time for Judas* and *A Wild Old Man on the Road*. According to the critics, *A Fine and Private Place* is either a delightful, ironic *roman à clef* or a pretentious, embarrassing self-indulgence. True to Callaghan's usual ambivalence of vision and form, it is probably a bit of both and therefore offers some useful insights into his long artistic career. This is a novel of mirrors in which Callaghan analyzes the writer Eugene Shore, who is remarkably similar to Callaghan and who proceeds to analyze "their" earlier novels — all of which demonstrate the problems of the intentional fallacy and of biographical criticism.

Al Delaney is a graduate student who, at the beginning of the novel, is experiencing the same sense of existential "loneliness" and worthlessness as Sam Raymond (*FP* 50). His academic training has taught him to impose a meaningful pattern on life and art through information and analysis:

> Information. Get all the information. He had the tool he trusted: analysis. He had never had any patience with mysteries. Everything could be explained. That's why he kept his journal, his notes about himself. All his training made him reject mysteries. (*FP* 21)

However, his relationship with Lisa Tolen suddenly disturbs his orderly, ambitious existence with a glimpse of all the mystery, wholeness, and "brightness of the world" in her "strange stillness" (*FP* 16). He finds he cannot use his "dreadful analytical habit" on her; she resists definition (*FP* 32).

By encouraging his interest in Eugene Shore, Lisa also indirectly leads him to question his commitment to "the graduate school . . . cop shop" where academics "pin [the writer] down, put the handcuffs on [his work]" (*FP* 88). Al decides to do a study of Shore's novels because, according to the critic Sharkey Kunitz (an Edmund Wilson figure), they have been so unjustly neglected in Canada (*FP* 36). But he finds that the scholarly "tools" taught him by Dr. Morton Hyland (a caricature of Northrop Frye) do not work on Shore's books. In a "joyous release" he realizes that in life and art "there are beautiful things that can't be explained" and a "magic" that unifies them (*FP* 62-63). Now "in love with a vision," compelled to enter all the vistas of Shore's thought, he refuses to commit his insights to any final form: "While a thing is unfinished, it is alive" (*FP* 127-29). He slowly moves out of Lisa's life and into Shore's world of art.

Al's analysis of Shore's works obviously provides Callaghan with an opportunity to reinterpret several of his earlier novels and emphasize some of his later concerns. Most of the images and themes are familiar to us. In Shore's "parables" of life, the "whole [work] is the symbol" and if "there's any magic it's in the way the imagination holds a life together" (*FP* 97). His heroes are clown-criminals "in the circus of life": their common denominator is that they are all "lovers knowing only the law of their own love" (*FP* 64-65). In order to achieve personal freedom, justice, independence — "their own being" — they inevitably come into conflict with the expectations of society (*FP* 78). In Shore's reversal of conventional values, "all the big law-and-order-men" ("Cops of the courts, cops of the church, political cops. Society's cops") are really just "respectable criminals," for the law is "an iron fence around the heart." And those that appreciate the mystery and love in life, "the artist and the saint," are "the last of the outlaws, holed up in the hills in some fine and private place" (*FP* 88, 101). This final image, with its allusion to "the grave" of Marvell's poem, ironically foreshadows Shore's unfortunate end.

Jason Dunsford is Callaghan's "law-and-order" representative. After a confrontation with Shore in which Jason plays a caricature of police brutality, he is more fully revealed as disappointed and frustrated, resentful of his powerlessness in his life and his job. When he reads one of Shore's novels (analogous to *Such Is My Beloved*), he decides that his loving concern for his wife's alcoholism has really put him on the same side as Shore and the "rascally, wrong-headed priests against their bishops, and whores and pimps too" (*FP* 107). Therefore, he painfully represses that love to put her into a sanatorium. When he needlessly kills the Panamanian boy, he waits "to be gripped by some terrible remorse" but only feels an "exalted, stunning sense of his own enlargement" and power (*FP* 121). Since the "cop with his gun is law and order" in society, Jason's crime is publicly vindicated despite the lack of "justice" (*FP* 172). Although Shore treats him "compassionately and fairly," he appears as a "pitiable thug" (*FP* 178). To defend his own egotism and desire for "power," his "exalted sense of himself as a man who knew that when things got out of order good people wanted them put right," Jason is, it is implied, responsible for Shore's death (*FP* 189).

Lisa Tolen, like Callaghan's earlier heroines, serves less as a realistic character and more as a metaphor for the theme and an analogue for his art. His original title for this story was "In the Dark and the Light of Lisa" (Staines, "Writer" 120). Shore says of her: "You don't need to bother reading [my novels]. You're in them" (*FP* 26). In her mysterious wholeness she has "a burning generosity of love" that receives Callaghan/Shore's benediction: "Whatever you are, whatever it is, you'll be forgiven. A girl like you always is. All through history you've been forgiven" (*FP* 148). However, unlike Anna Prychoda, Julie Evans, and even Peggy Sanderson, Lisa is basically self-centred and possessive in the dark side of her love. She is as fearful of her violent passions as she is of her existential emptiness:

> Unless she could love someone with all the fullness of her being, she became ruthless and destructive. And now, telling herself Al had gone for good, and feeling emptied, she wished she could believe in something outside her own life. She wished she could be a Marxist or a Calvinist or a Catholic. But the people she knew who had these fantasies had always bored her. (*FP* 134)

When Al leaves her, she accuses Shore of demoralizing him. Then, ruled only by her destructive passions, she betrays Shore to Jason. After Shore is killed, her "terrible cry for absolution" seems to come from a mysterious power outside her which demands her "remorse" (*FP* 192). She realizes that she has also betrayed Al's "independence, his defiance, his pursuit of his own vision, with her tragic meddling," and she confronts the spiritual "darkness" and universal sin within her ("It's in everybody," she whispered. "It must be"). However, instead of confessing (like Dostoevski's "pious penitents" whom Al scorns), she accepts her "torment" as a sacrifice for Al and decides to "make something out of it good for both of them" (*FP* 201-3). At the end she feels "carried along in a pattern that had its strange rightness" and "perfection" and "terrible beauty" (*FP* 207-8). Her love, like art, has given form to the mystery of life, uniting the dark and the light. She is blessed by "all ruthless, ripening nature for letting her love have its own law" (*FP* 213).

Al's final analysis of Shore's work is a metafictional summary of Callaghan's aesthetic. In a passage similar to parts of *That Summer in Paris* (*TSP* 21-22, 148), Shore describes his creative process as: "all of me hanging together, receptive just to the thing as it was — and the wonder of it — being just as it was. The wonder of separate things. . . . Not thinking about myself, I seemed to come all together" (*FP* 164). The result of this "heightened sense of life" is a sense of "mystery," the "mystification" of life that is "held together" in an art form by the "imagination" (*FP* 77, 164). Al extends Shore's "moments of wonder" at "the reality of things" to his characterization: his acceptance and "benediction" of those "self-directed exiles from society . . . where he offered them warmth and respect for being just what they were" (*FP* 164). Nevertheless, Al comes to realize that, while Shore's moral indulgence of these criminal-saints who pursue the law of their love could lead to "complete anarchy," it is balanced by what I have called Christian humanism (Maritain's "integral humanism") in Callaghan's work

which redeems "the rotten human stuff " (*FP* 142) of fallen nature with divine
love:

> There's the whole damned mystery. For some mysterious reason, it's
> something more than anarchy. I think I know why. I think it's some kind of
> warmth or love he has for all his characters, big or small, a love and respect
> for the mystery of the dignity of their personalities.(*FP* 197)

In Shore's "church" of the imagination all the outlaws are given dignity and
self-respect, "free to become aware of the adventurous possibilities of their
mysterious personalities" (*FP* 200-1).

This final analysis, however, does not resolve the moral ambiguities of
this novel. As Ina Ferris points out, "the supremacy of love as its 'own law'
[i]n *A Fine and Private Place* . . . means murder" (15). Another critic,
however, casually observes: "a social law has been violated, but fulfilment
has come through letting 'love have its own law'" (Bartlett 68), as if a hit-
and-run homicide is the moral equivalent of unconventional etiquette. Was
Shore's well-intentioned influence on the other three characters, in person and
through his novels, ultimately good or destructive? Is his death a result of
anarchical passions or divine pattern? By what standards do we judge or
differentiate between the actions of the heroine Lisa and the villain Jason?
And what about Shore himself? The "consoler" and "redeemer" (*FP* 182), he
is killed, buried "three days" later (*FP* 193), and it is finally asked "Are you
sure he's dead?" (*FP* 211). Shore's death is as ambiguous as those of his
"criminal saints."

Faced with these mysteries, a fashionable lack of closure, the rhetoric
of inclusiveness for fallen human nature, and an appeal to non-judgemental
Chekhov (*FP* 133), the critic may seem perverse to demand that the artist
reveal a coherent "pattern" in the "mystery" of reality through the
"wholeness" of his "imaginative vision." Nevertheless, this desire for artistic
meaning does not imply rigid academic categories or conventional moral
judgements; it is simply an expectation that Callaghan himself has invited in
the exhaustive repetition of these words as rhetorical motifs in his novel.
Near the end, Al articulates what seems to be Callaghan's position:

> Life is big enough and mysterious enough and bewildering enough and there
> are no final answers about it. None at all. Only questions. So you can make
> absolutely anything you want to make out of life. You'll be hit on the head,
> of course, by the authorities, who have agreed to make their own thing of it.
> But what the hell. You know they themselves are only making what they
> need to make to keep their authority. (*FP* 199)

In denying authoritarian absolutes, Callaghan is not, however, opting
for philosophical nihilism and moral relativism. Apparently he is reinforcing
his lifelong testimony that it must be the artist's unique vision that "makes"

something meaningful and coherent out of human experience. He discussed this responsibility at about the same time as he was writing this novel:

> Just information. Just technology. Outer space and inner despair. Yet it is the artist in words, or in paint or sculpture or in music who has a sense of form; in the glory of form is a sense of eternity. In short, it is the artist alone in this wild babble of information who tries to give some meaning to life. ("excerpt" 20)

Nevertheless, he has not fulfilled his own mandate in this novel, and the artistic incongruity is largely a product of the moral ambiguity, for Callaghan has consistently linked his "parables" to a moral vision.

In his 1973 interview with Donald Cameron, Callaghan defends his "own peculiar view of morality, [his] own sense of moral order in the world" (29). This statement is prefaced by his remarks about "disinterested goodness, the imaginative awareness of the wholeness of things" which "is mixed up in man's art, and often in his religion" and leads to passionate "excesses." This passion must be coupled with an "awareness of right action" and "love," not of "the idea," but of "human beings," for "if you know nothing about human love . . . you can't know anything about divine love" (22-23). Therefore, although his morality is "anarchistic in the sense that it is fiercely dependent upon the individual view never yielding to another man's sense of rectitude" (29-30), it is not without standards apparently compatible with Christian humanism. Even Jacques Maritain defines his individualistic saints thus:

> The saints always amaze us. Their virtues are freer than those of a merely virtuous man. Now and again, in circumstances outwardly alike, they act quite differently from the way in which a merely virtuous man acts. . . . They have their own kind of mean, their own kinds of standards. But they are valid only for each one of them. (*Existence and the Existent* 55)

The problem is that, in the context of Callaghan's later novels, this spiritual independence becomes a humanistic inclusiveness that sanctions murder and rape with no artistic indicators to discriminate between iconoclastic love and ruthless egocentricity.

Close to the Sun Again (1977) is a thinner novel than its predecessor, but it repeats many of the same basic themes (it also gives an interesting reprise of the central relationship in *The Loved and the Lost*). The moral of the novel is stated clearly at the end: "there could be no life, no love, no truth, without the passion that shattered all the rigid things" (*CS* 168). This is the passionate commitment to the wonder of life and the mystery of people that has distinguished all of Morley Callaghan's work. And he seems particularly to prize it as he grows older: "So you need these tensions, these passions, these frantic beliefs, these obsessions, the crazy fervour in young people. It's just too bad that as you grow older you get beaten up" (D. Cameron, "Callaghan" 24).

He also realizes (in an allusion to Yeats's "Easter 1916") that "the terrible beauty in the excess" of these passions (*CS* 168) can be destructive of the self and others, but, after almost fifty years of being the advocate of passionate sinner/saints, he stills seems to believe the risk is worth it.

Ira Groome, the hero of this novel, is a man without passions. As "The Commander" he has ruled his wife, his son, and his financial empire without "personal involvements" (*CS* 2). In his "impersonal, almost mechanical courtesy" to everyone and his "workmanlike," unsentimental sex with his mistress, he is practically inhuman (*CS* 14-15). Repeatedly, in the first fifty pages of this novel, he is characterized as a man of restraint, discipline, prudence, and proper appearances, in other words Callaghan's archetypal "boss of all the cops" (*CS* 23).

However, since his wife's death, Ira has been haunted by "voices in his own heart" out of a past he has deliberately repressed (*CS* 2). He has an uneasy sense of life passing him by, of "going downhill" from some forgotten "high point" (*CS* 32). Alienated from his respectable colleagues because they lack passion, knowing "nothing of a beauty born in excess," he begins to dream, with a sense of expectation, of a dark, enchanted place where "lawless men and women, holed up somewhere, [nursed] passions that made life so real" (*CS* 5). Then his mistress, Carol, echoes the words from the past that open the floodgates of memory: "Come back here, you bastard" (*CS* 52). Soon after, dying in a hospital emergency ward, Ira recalls the traumatic events leading up to the turning point in his life in a flashback that forms the last two-thirds of the novel.

When young Lieutenant Ira Groome first meets Gina Bixby and Jethroe Chone, the survivors of a U-boat attack who are picked up by his corvette, he himself has just recovered from a near-fatal wounding. His gratitude for and "wonder" at life give him an openness and "personal interest" in people (*CS* 60). As he gets to know Gina, he tells her about his former life as an archaeology student and the reason he had decided to give up the work of gravedigging "garbage" for the "enchantment" of life with a native girl (*CS* 80). He also relates the girl's ancient, existential wisdom (which recalls Al's remark near the end of the previous novel): "How they used to look at the world; cruel and senseless, a nightmare, always was, and always will be, and all we can do is make something beautiful out of the nightmare" (*CS* 81). However, Ira, still part of the "disciplined naval world," and searching for his own identity, is unequipped to understand the nightmare "world of violent personal passions" in which Gina and Chone struggle (*CS* 121). He has lived too much of his life as a "gravedigger" (*CS* 128).

Gina is caught in a desperate struggle between the two worlds within her, represented by Ira and Chone. Her "pride" and her "view of herself" demand Chone's death (*CS* 125) and make her gravitate toward Ira's world.

She identifies herself with "the magic city" of Tula, which he describes as "a place of light. All through history these links of light in the dark chain of history" (*CS* 106). However, deep within her, symbolized by "the sea and the jungle" and the "dark, threatening forest" in her eyes and "the dark roots of her blonde hair" (*CS* 106, 95), her "fatal flaw," her "wild, reckless nature" terrifies her (*CS* 122-23). Jethroe Chone, on the other hand, has a mysterious wholeness. In his "faith that he was right and had seen the ultimate pattern of things, [he] had a kind of criminal grandeur." His rape of Gina has translated his "passion" into "power" and "meaning," and his knowledge of "the core of her being" binds her to him (*CS* 123, 128).

The crisis comes on the life-float after their ship is sunk. Still struggling against her passionate and destructive "beauty" (with allusions to Yeats's "No Second Troy"), Gina clings to Ira for confirmation of her "real" nature (*CS* 154). Nevertheless, in the end, Chone's intense love and knowledge of her bind them in a fatal love-hate relationship: "No one wanted her more than I did. No one knew more about her than I did. No one looks up to her more than I did. No one loved her more than I did" (*CS* 155). When Chone rolls himself back into the sea, Gina dives after him calling "come back, you bastard" like "a woman with three kids who catches her husband running out on her" (*CS* 156-57).

After their deaths, Ira is tormented by the complex mystery of their lives: his "sure secret knowledge" of Gina's love for him (*CS* 158) and her cry that haunts him, demanding "the absolution of sympathetic compassion" for her betrayal of him (*CS* 164). Therefore, he silences his confusions with the deliberate rationalization that Gina deluded herself about her real nature until the moment she chose Chone:

> Gina hadn't been able to conceive of herself belonging to Jethroe Chone. Her fierce pride, her whole sense of herself, was violated by her passion for him, and so there was a secret torment in her, and she tried to believe she loved a man named Ira Groome. She tried very, very hard, even to the point of believing she wanted to see Chone killed, and she did not face what was in her heart until the last moment, when Chone tried to take himself away from her. (*CS* 164)

However, still "baffled" because "he suspected . . . he hadn't got her right," Ira now regrets his "childlike wonder," his belief that "even the jungle terror of deep personal involvements could be wonderful, could bring him more of the intoxication of life." As the doctor told him: "You got too close to the sun. That's all right. But if you get too close to people, you'll find they eat you up, and there won't be anything left of you." Therefore, he dedicates himself to the controlled, impersonal life of a naval officer (symbolized by the dead officer beside him in sick bay) and forgets "the wonder" of life and "the voices in his heart" (*CS* 164-66).

Remembering now as he is dying, Ira repents this "high treason" against "his own nature," the "protective habit" that over the years has withered his heart. And he finally confronts the truth about Gina and Chone:

> Chone . . . had all the passion. He tried to keep Chone's face in his mind so he could feel some of the terrible excess of his passion, the terrible beauty in the excess, because Chone knew the truth about himself in the power and intensity of his passion. The truth in the passion, as he should be able to see it now. As Gina had known. He saw now that there could be no life, no love, no truth without the passion that shattered all the rigid things. (*CS* 167)

The "perplexity and the mystery of people that made up the real adventure in life" mean that human passions may be darkly, terribly destructive, but they are also the light and fuel for all truly human endeavours. As Callaghan's favourite image, the circus parade of clown criminal-saints, comes marching again into Ira's heart, he finally achieves self-awareness. "Again close to the sun," he surrenders to peaceful death in the image of the "white leopard" (*CS* 167-69) — an allusion to T.S. Eliot's "Ash Wednesday" (cf. *CS* 122), but presumably also a symbolic union of Peggy Sanderson's snow white church and dark leopard — the lover has finally kept faith with his mysterious mistress.

Although this adventure story unfolds swiftly, expertly, with compelling suspense and vivid descriptions, it is basically unbelievable in premise, plot, and characterization. Several threads, such as the literary name-dropping and the Yucatan incident, are not well integrated. But the biggest problem is the apparent inconsistency in the symbolic values assigned to the prominent images of light and darkness, a difficulty also present in *A Fine and Private Place*. Presumably Callaghan is emphasizing the duality of human nature, and in these last two novels he seems to have changed his focus from the "gleams of heavenly light" to "the darkness of what we call evil forces" (Weaver 23). This is a valid artistic vision, although it does not inspire in us the same affection for his characters as we felt in his earlier novels. However, the lack of any clear religious or moral perspective in these novels further aggravates Callaghan's perennial problem of "moral flabbiness." We have reached the point at which we not only "misjudge and rejudge and misjudge his characters over and over again" (M. Wilson 79), but in fact suspect them of rape, murder, and other ruthless, selfish, and demonstrably unsaintly acts.

Despite Callaghan's rhetoric of non-judgemental characterization and unconventional morality, we do judge the "excesses" of his characters' passions when they inflict a very non-loving destruction on another human being in the name of love. It is not merely a "rigid" social conformity that objects to murder or rape, or refuses to celebrate them because Shore's death is part of a "pattern" that now guarantees his literary apotheosis (*FP* 208), and

Gina's rape binds her to Chone as his passions "overwhelmed" her (*CS* 114);
does that mean "she said no, but she really wanted it"?). Patricia Morley
represents the typical reader response: "These figures from the seventies are
both amoral and immoral. . . . They are canonized simply on the strength of
their passionate intensity and personal love . . ." (11). Ferris is more
judgemental: "This is an extreme and disturbing affirmation of the primacy of
the self, but there is no trace of irony . . ." (16). And Kendle concludes:
"[Callaghan's] vision is more romantic than tragic, the cult of passion, truth,
and wildness in opposition to dedicated service. And one wonders about the
validity of such a choice" (143). In his novels of the seventies, Callaghan has
portrayed the "nightmare" of human experience with terrible beauty and
passionate truth, but in his immersion in existential humanism, he has lost the
moral and religious illumination which once gave his fiction "the glory of
form" and "sense of eternity."

6. The truth of the story: *A Time for Judas, Our Lady of the Snows,*
A Wild Old Man on the Road

Callaghan published a final trilogy of novels before his death in 1990. In
them he reiterated (often with metafictional self-reflexivity) the perennial
religious themes of his fiction as they had become defined in an increasingly
secular form during the 1970s. Although his first novel of the 1980s, *A Time
for Judas*, amazed the secular critics with its overtly Christian subject matter,
its clear departure from biblical orthodoxy prompted one Catholic scholar to
label it "a death-dealing absurdity" (Dooley, "Love" 25). Callaghan's last
novels provide a summary and closure for his fiction by articulating a
theological basis for both his humanistic compassion and his aesthetic
principles. But it is clearly a theology that finds its ground of being in
humanity's divine nature rather than God's transcendent grace. The result,
legitimately, may be poor faith (Dooley's point) but persuasive fiction (in her
review, Helen Hoy applauded *A Time for Judas* as "a marked improvement
over [Callaghan's] recent novels" [329]). However, in his obvious desire to
provide meaningful answers to life's existential dilemmas, Callaghan's
evocation of the problems is more convincing than his sentimental solutions.

 A Time for Judas (1983) was, for Callaghan, a unique departure from
fifty-five years of urban realism: an historical-religious romance set primarily
in first century Jerusalem. Using the (rather trite) device of a "manuscript
found in a Greek jar" for verisimilitude, the novel purports to be a "true"
revision of the Gospel story of Christ's crucifixion and resurrection. It
supposedly resolves an inconsistency in the original story which depends on
Judas Iscariot's betrayal of Jesus:

> Nobody had to lead the guard to the Galilean's place and point him out.
> Everybody in the city knew where he was. And everybody knew the

Galilean, and what he looked like. No one had to point him out. . . . the
story doesn't make sense. (*TJ* 71-72)

The "truth" which "had a wonder and mystery [and] . . . grandeur of its own"
(*TJ* 245-46) is that Judas only "betrays" Christ out of love and obedience to
Him because "the story requires it" (*TJ* 125).

In fact, in a city whose large population was swelled by "as many as
100,000 pilgrims" for Passover (*International Dictionary of the Bible* 3:664),
even a very popular rabbi would not be known and recognized, in a pre-
television era, by "everybody," nor would the location of his private dinner
party be common knowledge (and it was important to capture him away from
his adoring mob). The logic of necessity for this biblical revisionism is no
more convincing than the device of a secret manuscript hidden for nineteen
hundred years, found by a scholar, destroyed by the Vatican, memorized by
an ex-Benedictine television producer, and conveyed to the implied author.
Nevertheless, it does provide the pretext for Callaghan's characteristic
rejection of "facts" and "authorities" in favour of "the power of the story" and
"the law of love." This Chinese box novel qualifies as historiographic
metafiction by foregrounding its fictionality (memory, notes, translated
language, distance, time), its intertexuality with the New Testament, and its
self-reflexive analysis of the cultural constructs and dynamic power of
storytelling. However, unlike most contemporary metafiction, the elaborate
foreword claiming authenticity, the lack of irony throughout, and the
vehement closure imposed by the narrator-scribe (who is portrayed as
immoral but not unreliable) do not allow for the rhetorical ambiguity often
characteristic of Callaghan. Neither, however, do they compel belief in either
the historical or the theological realm.

The Gospel according to Judas that emerges when "the time was right
for an end to the unbearable loneliness of Judas in the minds of all men on
earth" (*TJ* 247) is found in a "Greek jar [which] had figures inset around it, a
maiden in happy flight from a youth reaching out for her" (*TJ* 4). The
obvious allusion to Keats's urn suggests the self-consciousness of Callaghan's
artifact and previews his thematic obsessions with "time," "truth," and
"beauty" in this novel. The manuscript, including Judas's narrative (*TJ* 115-31),
is written by Philo, a Cretan Greek working in Jerusalem as a scribe to the
governor, Pontius Pilate. As agent for his father-in-law, a corrupt Roman
senator, he has been exiled for illegal profiteering and desperately awaits
recall by this man in whom all of his "faith" in all of his "judgements" resides
(*TJ* 12). In the meantime, he becomes involved in both Jewish society and the
Roman garrison and has a front-row seat for the climax of the story: the trial,
crucifixion, and resurrection of "the Galilean," Jesus of Nazareth.

Philo functions well as Callaghan's typical alter ego: urbane, cynical,
philosophical and literary, sexually liberated, and, most important, attracted to

iconoclasts and "outlaws." Some of his aesthetic statements are pure Callaghan (an elaborate explanation is given for the anachronistic colloquialisms [*TJ* 6], but it does not excuse the numerous rhetorical and historical errors):

> [A]ll this talk in Jerusalem about "as it was written." Too much poring over the meaning of the word, the meaning of the meaning, then the meaning behind the meaning. When I hear someone say "as it was written," I say cynically, "Well, who wrote it and why?" (*TJ* 160)

Several critics have taken this as Callaghan's denunciation of academic criticism and his plea for transparency of artistic meaning (Carr 311). This interpretation is somewhat inconsistent, however, with a novel obsessed with the complexity of truth and the power of story. Philo's cynicism is mostly directed against Callaghan's perennial villains — the authorities who try to control people's hearts and destroy their "sacred private domain" (*TJ* 238) with legalistic codes and rules (Eugene Shore would have called them "the cops" of Judaism). Philo, with his symbolic Greek name, represents the antithesis of legalistic bondage — the freedom of love which he practises avidly in his many sexual liaisons, often liberating women who are mere chattels of the marriage contract (*TJ* 8). Philo also demonstrates remarkable parallels, probably not coincidental, with his namesake, the Hellenistic Jewish philosopher (c. 20 B.C. – A.D. 50) who espoused an eclectic variety of doctrines, especially a Greek allegorization of Jewish Scripture and a concentration on the Logos which greatly influenced Johannine and patristic concepts of Christ (*Oxford Dictionary of the Christian Church*).

To Pilate, Philo articulates an elaborate psychological critique of the Jewish faith which requires the Atonement, and therefore Judas's betrayal. This theme is stressed, apparently without irony, throughout the novel and verges uncomfortably on anti-Semitism. The "Jewish mind," captive in "the desert" of its origin and sojourn, is "land-locked," "isolated, lonely," and existentially alienated (in contrast to the Greeks whose life on "the sea" produces spiritual and intellectual "freedom" and "curiosity"). As a result, the Jews psychologically project "fantastic mirages" (symbolized by the "flaming flowers" of the desert): a "Yahweh . . . in their own minds . . . so they can have a feeling of being chosen even in their desert isolation." Since "Yahweh was merely the collective consciousness of the Jews," they have to "control themselves" through the elaborate rules and rituals of "Yahweh's law book" arbitrated by "the priests." The result is "a subjugation of all that's spontaneous in the heart. . . . The perfect captivity" (*TJ* 142-44).

Moreover, according to the law, Yahweh must be appeased with the "sacrificial blood" (*TJ* 84) of an innocent victim, and the Messiah becomes the mythological substitute for the usual lamb (*TJ* 17): "people wouldn't go on believing in him unless he fitted into the great myth of death and resurrection" because "the story requires it" (*TJ* 124-25). Therefore, because Judas represents the quintessential duality of humanity, possessing "more of the human chaos, rage, hate, anger, selfishness, pride, meanness, generosity, love. More love for him . . . ," he is "used by the Son of God, picked to be the victim" who will betray Jesus (*TJ* 130-31). However, this archetypal betrayal is intended by Christ to shatter the codes of Judaism and simultaneously enact and subvert the traditional "story":

> The story as it had been written, yes, his followers needed it. The law, its codes. But he himself had said, "Judge not." For him there was only one law — love. Then maybe only one source of all evil — betrayal. The whole inner world [Callaghan's "private domain"] swinging between love and betrayal. . . . (*TJ* 125)

Here, Philo's inscription of Judas's interpretation of Christ's theology is, of course, Callaghan's perennial theme: the only law, truth, or theology is love (*TJ* 132, 231: "It's all you need to know" would seem to supersede even Keats's beauty).

Although a shadowy figure in the novel (literally so in the Resurrection), Jesus represents Callaghan's archetypal hero: "God in man," "and in everyone alive," the ultimate "storyteller," isolated, mysterious, magical, full of "awareness," "compassion," and imagination, "bent on overthrowing the real masters of the world," and "freeing [humanity] from the heavy bondage of the law" so everyone can make his/her own "choice" about "the right action" for "each situation" (*TJ* 119-23). He is Callaghan's quintessential "outlaw," extrapolated from Scripture but emphasizing humanism, iconoclasm, and situational ethics much more than orthodox theology. Significantly, he is also the lover of Mary Magdalene who represents love (*TJ* 230) and the saviour of Mary of Samaria, the "sacred whore," who represents beauty (*TJ* 61). According to this biblical revision, the two Marys were censored and conflated by the early Christians into one figure with better public relations value.

This novel is constructed of elaborate parallels and doubles. Philo's friend and counterpart is Judas, iconoclast and outsider (*TJ* 17), lover and betrayer; Philo's "master" is Simon the Idumaean who is paralleled to Jesus. Simon is also liberated from the Jewish laws and superstitions; he "owed it to his own self-respect to be an outlaw" (*TJ* 39-40). Facing death on a cross beside Jesus (*TJ* 168), he never betrays Philo's faith in him (although there is "no reason why Simon should suffer and die for me" [*TJ* 77]) and represents a kind of "grace" in the love, trust, and freedom he offers his friend (*TJ* 58), despite the element of "betrayal" within Philo, as in all humanity (*TJ* 104). The double crucifixion is the most moving, effective scene in the novel and compensates for some apparently pointless anachronisms in the Passion story (such as the insertion of eight extra days between Maundy Thursday and Easter Sunday).

Up to this point, Callaghan has basically dressed his usual characters in period costume. But, in the story of the Resurrection he attempts to integrate religion and realism in an episode unique in his fiction. Unlike Graham Greene, for example, who incorporated supernatural acts (divine intervention and epiphanies) into his religious fiction, Callaghan has always grounded his narratives in the natural world. The appearance of the risen Jesus to Philo (after he has assisted in the body-snatching from the now-"empty tomb") tries to cover all theological positions without clarifying any: it is neither the physical resurrection of orthodoxy nor the spiritual manifestation of liberal theology:

> His grave was there, undisturbed, though I had seen him here last night, . . . and it couldn't have been just a vision, for Isaiah had seen him, too. So, something more than a vision. I'm not saying he was flesh and bone, a body coming out of the grave. Yet he was real. . . . Yet not of this flesh. So something of another substance that as yet we do not know. (*TJ* 218)

The theology may be imprecise, but, more importantly for Callaghan, it gives grounds for a repetition of his aesthetic of the holy in the daily, the word made flesh:

> And it didn't matter where the Galilean's bones were. They weren't needed in his new bright enlargement. While my wonder grew, I had a sense of reality widening as I looked around, with everything — trees, rocks, the horse, the nearby vineyard, even the sky — coming so close that they hurt and brought tears to my eyes. As Judas had said in his story, I now saw that the Galilean in his magic substance could be all around me. (*TJ* 219)

As theodicy, the ending of *A Time for Judas* is trite and sentimental: "Where is he? Where there's love" (*TJ* 231). As aesthetic theory, it foregrounds self-reflexivity and ambiguity in its debate between "the story" and "the truth" (*TJ* 220, 240-42), yet ultimately settles, without apparent irony or narrative subversion, for one version of "the truth," suppressed by both authority and charity, but ultimately prevailing in its unvarnished "story" (*TJ* 147).

As usual, Callaghan is most interested in morality, the application of his religious principles to life. Again, in a corrupt and fallen world, the personal integrity of the individual ("self-respect," "inner light," "private domain") must never be betrayed, and the guiding principle for that "secret domain" is not the rules of church or society or even objective "truth" ("Is the truth ever a betrayal? I wondered. Yes, one man can rat on another. The informer? The eternal rat" [*TJ* 245]). The only law is love which, for Callaghan, means the divine incarnate in humanity. The moral ambiguity that we noted in previous novels, in which the law of love resulted in rape and murder, has achieved its ultimate expression in this book with the ultimate sin — the betrayal and murder of God himself. Callaghan attempts to justify this act by asserting eternal providence behind Judas' motivation. However, neither the superficial theology (to be fair, it did take Milton twelve books to resolve this problem), nor the blame-the-victim morality convinces the reader of Callaghan's exoneration of Judas.

Our Lady of the Snows appeared in 1985 as a new novel "suggested by the story The Enchanted Pimp" (cover blurb). It is actually a much-revised story that Callaghan began in 1963 as "Thumbs Down on Julien Jones"; published in Exile in 1973 as "The Meterman, Caliban and Then Mr. Jones" (also a CBC film in 1974); issued as a novella, The Enchanted Pimp (with No Man's Meat) in 1978; expanded with two further chapters in Exile in 1979 (now called The Stepping Stone); and finally published with nine additional chapters as a "new" novel (Boire 82). The most significant plot amendment is the ending. Ilona's murder in chapter 13 of The Enchanted Pimp becomes, almost word for word, Daphne's murder in Chapter 10 of Our Lady of the Snows; at the end of the novel, Ilona is living happily ever after. As Callaghan self-reflexively says in this novel, "it was as if [he] had to keep changing the story a little, changing it till [he] got it in the right shape" (OL 173).

Structurally, the expansion of the novella adds interesting characters, subplots, and detailed urban texture, but the literary padding seriously detracts from the unity and coherence of the novel. The subplots concerning Gil Gilhooley (Chapter 6), the judge (Chapter 9), Robert and Marika (Chapter 12), and several other minor stories have a tangential thematic relevance (usually dealing with "love" versus "the law" [OL 82]) but are not integrated into the main plot. The literary allusions are pretentious and unconvincing (OL 60, 135). And the ominous foreshadowings of Ilona's murder (OL 52, 92), after it is transferred to Daphne halfway through the book, appear as manipulative red herrings in view of her impossibly romantic fate. This book is not vintage Callaghan, but it is an interesting reprise-and-variation on several of his earlier urban morality tales: the prostitute and pimp from Such Is My Beloved; the mystery woman and enchanted/confused man from The Loved and the Lost; the icon and her mentor from A Passion in Rome (the scene in Muldoon's is reminiscent of Carla's disastrous debut). As I have argued, the characters have become more secularized than those of the 1930s novels — the male saviour in this novel is a pimp not a priest, and the salvation he offers is material not spiritual. However, the duality of good and evil within humanity seems to have become unrealistically gender-polarized. This sexist simplification may be a result of Callaghan's developing conviction that "women have to be on the side of life more than men because of the way they function" (D. Cameron, "Callaghan" 25). Callaghan's female icons have always been characterized by their non-puritanical, non-legalistic, sexual generosity; his female equivalent of the male "outlaw" may be the prostitute, or, at least, the mistress. Consequently, while the heroine is technically a whore, she has a perfect heart of gold (like Mary of Samaria and Mary Magdalene), and the male protagonist (while more sympathetic than Lou) is not the naively flawed Father Dowling, Jim McAlpine, or Sam Raymond, but a cynical thug (*OL* 22, 141) and cold-blooded murderer (*OL* 192).

Edmund J. Dubuque, nicknamed Da Boot because of his symbolic imperfection, a clubfoot, is not totally without sympathy for the reader; Callaghan has embraced him in his church of the imagination. He is a petty gangster and a pimp for bored housewives, but he is also a loving husband and father-to-be with literary interests and a sentimental streak (he gives charity to a destitute family). Typically for Callaghan, it is through this male centre of consciousness that we see the theme unfolding around the heroine's static significance: the pimp dynamically develops in his understanding from a cynical stereotyping of women to an enchanted "wonder" at the "mystery" of the "golden whore" (*OL* 209).

In the beginning, Dubuque is characterized as one of Callaghan's blessed outlaws by "his fierce sense of himself in the face of death" (*OL* 35). His flaw is a simplistic division of women into absolute categories: "He had come to believe that a woman was either born to be a saint and didn't know it, or a whore and didn't know it, but it was up to him to know, and he thought he did know" (*OL* 19). However, Ilona Tomory represents the saintly whore, "a woman he didn't understand at all" (*OL* 43). With the dignity and self-respect of a "princess," she dispenses her favours to "the lame, the halt, and the blind" (the connection with Dubuque is obvious) (*OL* 41). She rejects the arrogant, exploitative men to offer a "gentle benediction," a "compassionate recognition" and "warmth of new life" to the "losers" and "nobodies" (*OL* 39). Biblical metaphors ("something of great price" [*OL* 42]) mark Dubuque's description of her absolution through love: "a fabulous whore, a natural with a strange gift for creating the great illusion that makes a man feel that no matter what he has done, if she touched him he would feel excused and comforted" (*OL* 43). Gil, the writer-bartender who functions as Callaghan's alter ego here, provides the theological theme which affirms incarnational humanism and denies dualistic rejection of the flesh: "there's as much mystery in dirt and dung as there is in heaven" (*OL* 40: a probable allusion to Yeats's "Crazy Jane Talks with the Bishop").

Like "an artist" who has "a fantastic sense of her own special value," associated with the aristocratic background of her family and the fur coat that is their talisman (*OL* 50-53), Ilona possesses a "gift" of "magic" and "wonder" that wraps men in an imaginative "illusion of intimacy" and "compassion" (these Callaghan code words for incarnational love and art echo throughout the novel: *OL* 90, 97, 122-23, 181). Therefore, Ilona represents the quintessence of the word made flesh in her profession: "fucking" is "sacramental . . . religious" and "the core of all mysteries" (*OL* 164, 195).

However, the men who compete for her, although they appreciate her "mystery," represent the two antithetical poles of the flesh and spirit dichotomy in their attempts to control and exploit her "magic." Ultimately, Dubuque is a materialistic pimp, and Johnny Sills is a spiritual "soul sucker" (*OL* 199). Gil, in contrast, as the "storyteller," is the only one who truly appreciates the grace and power of her myth.

Despite Dubuque's rhetoric about helping women ("all I wanted was to give a girl a far better life" [*OL* 158]), his relations with them are primarily commercial and exploitative. He "didn't understand" Ilona because "everything had a price," and with this "big-bucks hooker," "something of great price was being thrown away, before his eyes" (*OL* 42-43). His "respect" for women consists of "[putting] a high price on them" (*OL* 162), and his cynicism concerning them is characteristic of the pimp: "Where does any woman go? Where the money is" (*OL* 148). His materialism is symbolized in his fur hat and coat collar (*OL* 36), the products of procurement for women who owe money on their fur coats (*OL* 21). Therefore, he is confused about the significance of Ilona's fur coat which represents, not material value, but family dignity and self-respect (for example, warming her mother as she dies [*OL* 169]). When he finds out the coat is commercially worthless under its proud exterior, he discounts it, as he discounts Ilona's compassion for men, as "just an illusion" (*OL* 181). However, his furrier friend helps him to see that the magic and illusion of human love can transform reality, and because of "the human thing about that coat" (its real significance), he offers to repair it as a "human being" — "Not as a furrier. As an artist" (*OL* 156). Although Ilona recognizes, as Gil does, that Dubuque's enchantment with her goes beyond the "ruthlessly commercial" (*OL* 160), his agenda for her still denies the spiritual reality that she finds in her "parents' home" and in Johnny Sills: "It's not your world, Dubuque. It's far away from you. It's a world I love now, a world where you could never be" (*OL* 185).

However, Johnny Sills, trying to "be an artist" and "give a shape to his life" (*OL* 184-85), represents the other extreme of the spirit/flesh dualism and proves equally unsatisfying. At the beginning, he "respects" Ilona for the "peace" and "dreams" she gives him (*OL* 184). But finally, like "a crazy monk," he rejects her human sexuality and tries to use her as "a stepping-stone" (the book's original title) to his "religious rainbows" (*OL* 198-201). In an echo of *That Summer in Paris*, Callaghan represents Sills as akin to the transcendentalist Wordsworth, rejecting the immediacy of experience (*TSP* 19-20), and he puts his rebuttal of "the terrible vanity of the artist who wanted the word without the flesh" (*TSP* 148) in Ilona's mouth:

> He said, "Ilona, for one kind of man. . . . 'A primrose by the river's brim a
> yellow primrose was to him — and nothing more.' I'm not that kind of

man," and I yelled, "What the hell's the matter with a beautiful primrose? You may know a lot about that big inner world of yours, but you don't realize the wonder of things around you. . . . I don't care about all this lofty mystical nonsense. The fact is you don't want to know anything about me." (*OL* 198)

Neither the "soul sucker" (*OL* 199) nor the materialist can fully apprehend "our lady of the snows"; she represents the unity of the snow on the mountain tops where "things come in flashes" (*OL* 40) and the snow in the streets (*OL* 52), the world of reality touched by "wonder" (*OL* 81). Only Callaghan's "story-teller" Gil can fully apprehend her: "in his imagination she kept taking on a larger life and different forms" (*OL* 189). Despite accusations of "sentimentality," Gil keeps faith with her myth (*OL* 210) and is rewarded by news of her romantic resolution. In the final chapter, the centre of consciousness changes to Gil who hears the "story" of "the princess" and the sailor from a mysterious "foreign" gentleman. Ilona has finally found a husband who, like her, combines "poetry" and "earthiness," and in the "magic" of their wholeness, they sail the seas of "wonder" and of "the rightness of things" — "the seas of God" (*OL* 212-15).

This "novel of real people, real streets, real life" (cover blurb) has ended as pure fairytale. The spiritual significance of "the seas of God" has lost most of the theological content that Callaghan, like Maritain, originally invested in the unity of "the word made flesh" (*TSP* 148). Instead, reality has been injected with sentimental romanticism and called blessed.

In Morley Callaghan's last novel, *A Wild Old Man on the Road* (1988), the self-referential recycling of former works and ideas is clearly deliberate: Callaghan said, "if I do get this right, it will be the one that throws light on what [I've] done before" (qtd. in Dunn 53). The result, reminiscent of *A Fine and Private Place*, is both naively self-serving and morally complex. The centre of consciousness is a young acolyte, Mark Didion (another Al Delaney). The interesting irony of this novel, however, is that the "wild old man," Jeremy Monk (a Eugene Shore clone), becomes a portrait of the anti-Christ, a Callaghan alter ego who ends up betraying all the Callaghan values and thereby justifies his creator who, we infer by contrast, was faithful to the end.

The novel is set in the late 1960s and portrays a generation, characterized by a "sense of personal freedom, the liberation of the spirit and of the person," supposedly analogous to "the artists of the twenties" whom Callaghan portrayed in *That Summer in Paris* (*WO* 6). Mark Didion is a representative of this generation, rebelling against an "arch-conservative" father who has sold out his former artistic ideals for the presidency of "a large advertising agency that held many government contracts" (*WO* 1). He insists that his son prostitute his writing talents for the family firm (the sixties clichés are as uncomfortably naive as

MacLennan's in *Return of the Sphinx*; the interesting difference is that Callaghan supports the opposite side of the generational gap from MacLennan). Mark, however, aspires to be a real journalist like his hero Jeremy Monk, who is concerned not with the personality cult of self-advertising journalism but "only with truthful reporting" (*WO* 5). In contrast with Mark's father, who could "turn his back so completely on the passion of his youth, even become someone else" (*WO* 13), this surrogate father has never committed that "sin against himself" (*WO* 23) but has remained true to his "secret domain . . . that faint secret unconquerable area of self-respect" (*WO* 16). This is the Callaghan code, illustrated in all his later novels and articulated defensively in his interview with Donald Cameron: the "inner glow" of youth gets replaced by "other people's view of things" if "anybody gets control of your purse," so it was always "*terribly* important to [him] as a writer" to be economically independent (19-20). In this morality tale, Callaghan demonstrates the destructive perils of violating his code when "the wild old man" goes "on the road."

After his father's death, Mark follows his memory to Montparnasse where he encounters his idol at the turning point of Monk's career, witnesses his downfall, overcomes his own "anxiety of influence," and eventually possesses the Oedipal prize, one of Callaghan's sexy saints. Until now, Monk "never went on tours or made these personal appearances that help sell a book and make a man a big public personality. Monk just lived for the truth that was in his work" (*WO* 20). His writing has been characterized not by the "fashionable . . . lifeless games" of "structuralism, post-modernism" but by "great and truthful reporting" (*WO* 40); above all he has given people "dignity and autonomy" in art and life (*WO* 38) by maintaining for himself and them the creed that "I am what I am" (*WO* 42) (this is probably intended to echo Yahweh [Exodus 3:14] not Popeye).

His "transparent" aesthetic, like Callaghan's, is a product of his theology, which celebrates the sensual, "the word made flesh":

> that dark Christian shadow about the whole sexual experience. . . . Well, it's a Christian aberration. . . . I think all this would have astonished the Galilean. It certainly didn't come from him. . . .The aberration was dignified as Christian asceticism. And I think this denial of our nature is a sad, pathetic, impudent rebuke to our creator. (*WO* 94-95)

Belying his name, Monk is portrayed as having a strong sexual appeal for women, particularly for the artist whom Mark loves, Cretia Sampari. She shares Monk's conviction that true realism is impressionism, as in Monet's paintings where nature is seen "for the first and only time as no one could ever see it again" (*WO* 48; compare Callaghan's praise of the impressionists: "Cezanne's apples. The appleness of apples. Yet just apples. . . . the way Matisse looked at the world . . . a gay celebration of things as they were. . . . The word made flesh" [*TSP* 148]).   Similarly, Monk's (and Callaghan's) "incarnational" reportage depends on a personal objectivity, the paradox of apprehending the holy in the daily: "It was, of course, a personal report. Was it objective? Was Flaubert objective? Was he the most highly objective or the most truly personal of all reporters? The question you should ask is: Was there truth in the observations?" (*WO* 62)   It is significant that Callaghan foregrounds the subjective constructions of narrative in this metafictional discussion, but at the same time makes a very non-post-modern appeal to the metaphysics of presence when he valorizes his writing as objective "truth" (*WO* 62).

The moral of this portrait of the artist as an old man lies in Monk's betrayal of Callaghan's creed. Seduced by money and fame, he abandons the "personal" for the cult of the "personality":

> I, as a writer, have kept to myself. I'm a private person. In the trade I've been in the intellectual ghetto. Not many readers. Well, I now want people to read me. In this crazy system there's only one way to do it. Become a personality, a figure. (*WO* 67)

Although Monk's first time "on the road" to "flog" his book (*WO* 43) allows Callaghan to satirize a number of contemporary targets, it also documents the writer's gradual deterioration until "he did not bother to talk about his books. Maybe he felt he didn't need to now that he had become a presence" (*WO* 98-99). Ironically, Monk chastises the famous "poet" (obviously Irving Layton) for his own crimes against the "sacred secret domain" of the writer and for the "self-indulgent" "freedom" that abandons "the glory of form . . . discipline . . . self-respect . . . truth" (*WO* 78).

Arrogantly, Monk now becomes a modern "Jeremiah, brooding and wailing over the sins of his own Jerusalem" (*WO* 59). He retreats into the Galilean "desert" and (in imagery echoing *A Time for Judas*) takes the "awful desolation" "deeper into the desert within himself" (*WO* 106-7). Mark, who is apparently supposed to guide the reader in moral judgement, tries to justify Monk by a loyalty to his old persona: "he tried to tell himself Monk had merely become a Christian socialist. He told himself Monk had come to believe in the dignity and importance of the person, and was seeing this as part of his old quest for a new and greater freedom" (*WO* 107), what Maritain would have called Christian humanism. However, Mark finally realizes his hero's self-betrayal of "the pattern set for his nature" (*WO* 112), and the betrayal of incarnational humanism, when Monk repudiates his former sensuality (the basis of his theology and his aesthetic) along with Mark's friendship (which has represented the faith in his old integrity). Quoting Gerard Manley Hopkins, whose work celebrated the sacred made sensual, Mark warns Cretia: "Glory to God for dappled things, Cretia, . . . I can say that when I'm with you. It's even in the warmth of your hand. Don't let him change you, Cretia" (*WO* 118).

In their "spiritual marriage . . . beyond sexual satisfaction," "St. Jeremy" has become a monk whose vanity converts aging disillusionment and impotence into spiritual polemics and conservative politics (*WO* 119-20, 126). This dualistic heresy is idealism as tyranny; it is "against life" and against art (*WO* 129-31). And the heresy of Monk's theology is denounced by Mark as destructive, neo-conservative warmongering:

> And this new freedom. Now it's [Monk] and God — if God will only let him get a little closer. Okay, he will! Yes he will, and he'll have a hundred thousand young men killed in the jungle to serve his moral purpose. A wild old man on a white horse riding at the head of his great new constituency. (*WO* 140)

Callaghan finally clarifies his authorial bias against Monk in this negative image of the "white horse" from *The Loved and the Lost*, and the pejorative association of Monk with Solzhenitsyn (*WO* 140) whom Callaghan had condemned as his fallen hero in an article written in 1983:

> [Solzhenitsyn was] willing to have a hundred thousand or two hundred thousand young men slaughtered for the sake of the triumph of his own faith. . . . All this for a war I didn't believe in myself. A man on a white horse! How those mounted men have driven that same white horse through the bloody fields of history. ("Christmas" 102)

Monk's "religious" and "celibate fantasies," associated with the desert, aim to violate Cretia's imagination and change her nature, as they have his own, so that "the fresh wonder of real things" which is art must atrophy (142-46). The contrast with Samuel Beckett, "the kind of private self-directed man Jeremy Monk had once been" (*WO* 153), provides Monk's artistic epitaph: he has become the "spiritual man" (*WO* 153) who represents "the terrible vanity of the artist who wanted the word without the flesh" (*TSP* 148). Interestingly, Callaghan does not point out now that the "godless" Beckett may create brilliant art, but it is hardly the "gay celebration of things as they were" to which Callaghan once aspired (*TSP* 148).

In an anachronistic reprise of *A Passion in Rome*, the death of the Holy Father sets the scene for the death of Mark's artistic and "spiritual father" (*WO* 165). Pride and greed have made Monk a "public figure" (*WO* 170), but in the "desolation" of the desert and the "emptiness" of human works, he has come to an existential awareness of his self-betrayal (*WO* 173-76):

> I had got too close to God. Now God could see me. God looked at me, Mark; I knew he didn't like what he saw. . . . Vanity, vanity, Mark. . . . The real thing is, a man must know what's right for him. A man must not sin against himself. (*WO* 176)

Having confronted his spiritual death, he commits physical suicide. In the beginning, he told Mark, "You die for the thing you live for" (*WO* 40). As he once survived suicide to "live for the truth" (*WO* 94), so he now dies for it: "opening a door into another room" (*WO* 181). The hope of the resurrection presumably resides in Mark and Cretia's love.

In this morality tale, the melodramatic plot, romanticized (and sexist) characterization, and dated social commentary subvert any pretext to realistic fiction. However, the ironic presentation of Jeremy Monk and the doubleness of vision introduced by the reader's identification with both him (obviously the author's doppelgänger) and Mark Didion (the reader's surrogate) add an interesting complexity and suspense to the novel, at least until Monk's heresy becomes clear about two-thirds of the way through the book. Despite some red herrings (like the suicide note), Callaghan seems didactically to invoke closure on the moral issue with Monk's recantation (*WO* 176).

The theological theme, however, remains more ambiguous. Although repeatedly invoked as a sanction for both truth in art and truth in life, Christian theology ("[God] didn't like what he saw") very quickly becomes humanistic integrity ("a man must know what's right for him") at the thematic epiphany (*WO* 176). Callaghan says some positive things about Chartres and Hopkins and some negative things about Solzhenitsyn, the pope, and "the celebrated Christian capitalist journalist" (*WO* 108). However, ultimately his theology has lost a Catholic, or even Christian, content that Jacques Maritain would have recognized, and has become a self-indulgent nostalgia that reduces humanism to egocentrism. Although Callaghan still invokes a metaphysics of presence to ground his final moral fables, no longer does his word give his incarnations of the flesh the power to persuade the reader of their truth morally or spiritually.

7. Conclusion: "the irreducible mysteriousness of life"

In tracing the development of Callaghan's faith through his fiction, I have suggested that there is a constant, unresolved tension between his religious vision and his fidelity to existential realism. Callaghan always had a profound commitment to portraying the mysterious and sometimes "rotten" stuff of human existence. And he always attempted, through his iconoclastic but basically religious view of life, to give reality some moral meaning and eternal significance. The ambiguous mixtures of the sacred and the secular in his novels are the result of this tension. The focus of his vision changed over his long career: from a tentative naturalism, to a Christian humanism concentrated at first most strongly in the metaphysical realm and later focused on the secular world, and finally to an emphasis on humanistic struggles almost devoid of theological illumination and form. As Desmond Pacey warned long ago, the defect of Callaghan's liberal Christian vision is moral flabbiness. I think his best novels are still the parables of the thirties, with their uneasy but significant tension between grace and nature, and the more realistic novels of mid-century which attempt to illuminate the diverse actions of the sacred within the secular. However, as his religious vision becomes less theocentric and logocentric in his later works, his novels become flabbier in both artistic form and moral meaning.

Nevertheless, throughout his career Callaghan portrayed the human struggle with compassionate sincerity and the ring of truth. He was not really a stylist; his fictional forms were always conventional, his structures and characterization often awkward, and his "transparent" prose more like "coarse-grained, serviceable burlap" (M. Wilson 82). He was, however, in the terms of this study, and, I suggest, in the context of modern Canadian literature, a major religious novelist. He met his sinner-saints in their limit-situations and dramatized their spiritual struggles in all the irreducible mysteriousness of life. He demonstrated the redemptive action of grace in the relations of humanity. And he never compromised his artistic responsibility to portray the existential questions by invoking an easy orthodoxy or imposing a dogmatic resolution.

Note

[1] Gary Boire, in his recent biography of Callaghan, *Literary Anarchist*, discloses a significant personal connection between Jacques Maritain and *Such Is My Beloved*:

From a letter written by Callaghan to Max Perkins on 3 September 1933, we know the true nature of the novel's conception and development. One evening at Avenue Road, when the conversation turned to the problem of prostitution, Maritain told the sad story of a young priest he knew back in Paris. The young man had befriended two prostitutes, tried to help them materially, but when the news broke and scandal erupted, the experience shattered his spirit. The priest had had a nervous breakdown and was now cloistered in a French monastery, deranged and broken-spirited. Maritain was personally saddened by these events, particularly since he'd known the young priest quite well.

At this point Callaghan was in the middle of a new novel, possibly an early draft of *They Shall Inherit the Earth*, which was published a mere twelve months after *Such Is My Beloved*. He had, in fact, already written over 30,000 words. But Maritain's anecdote affected him so powerfully that he abandoned this work-in-progress and, in a "grand passion," wrote *Such Is My Beloved* between late February or early March and May 1933 (Letter to Perkins, 14 June [1933]). (68)

IV

A SPECULATIVE CONCLUSION: FICTION AND FAITH

[T]he true vocation of the poet and the writer [is] to portray reality in toto, that is, to portray life with that integral natural-supernatural realism which François Mauriac had demanded. This vocation might — in an age of faith — have coincided with the spirit of the age. In an age of skepticism, nonbelief, cynicism and despair, it is all the more incumbent upon the writer to remain loyal to his vocation, taking, if necessary, his stand resolutely against the spirit of the age, without flinching and without compromise. (Reinhardt 237)

I have considered the problematic relationship between fiction and faith in this post-Christian era with particular reference to Hugh MacLennan and Morley Callaghan, the two most important Canadian novelists of the first half of this century. Their solutions to the problem of the religious novel have been very different and, in both cases, not entirely successful. Inevitably, some points of comparison have emerged along the way, and, as I suggested in my Introduction, their respective patterns of religious fiction may reflect and illuminate one another.

The most significant similarity, of course, arises from their religious worldview. These novelists of the modern era did not share the modernist perception that life is horrifying, absurd, or meaningless; for them it was part of a larger purpose that invests it with dignity and value. Because the world has been redeemed in time, and grace is acting in nature, creation has truth and beauty, actions and decisions have ultimate worth, and human self-realization must include a spiritual element because our destiny is part of an eternal pattern. This Christian humanism is the source of the generally optimistic attitude and confident tone which we find in these writers. It is also reflected in their "traditional" and transparently realistic, rather than experimental or problematized, writing styles: linear narrative, concrete description, omniscient or reliable voice, consistent characterization, and a sense of stable, objective reality in their settings.

But, there are also distinctive differences between these novelists, in part emerging from their respective theological positions. MacLennan's logocentric fiction is a product of the Protestant Augustinian tradition of Platonic dualism, idealism, and subjectivism. It privileges the Word but rejects the world. Again, to quote the Anglican critic, Malcolm Ross: "Protestant theology rejected the doctrine of transubstantiation, denied the 'real presence,' and allegedly cut off the created world, so that it could no longer be a valid bearer of divine meaning" (qtd. in Wilder 86-87). Unable to transubstantiate nature into the supernatural, Protestant writers tend toward both a transcendent, vaporous spirituality and a subjective, individualistic revelation. This aesthetic does not facilitate an inclusive fictional representation. Consequently, we find that MacLennan often imposes a theoretically divine solution onto the personal struggles of his characters or else arbitrarily transports their physical conflicts into the metaphysical realm.

In contrast, Callaghan has inherited the Aristotelian-Thomist tradition of hylomorphism (form within matter), the doctrine of divine immanence. To reiterate Wilder, "The Roman doctrine of transubstantiation in the Mass is the key to Catholic art. It defines the relation of grace to nature, and the relations of the Catholic artist to the world" (85-86). The greatest religious novelists of this century have been Catholic. Their answer to the problem Reinhardt poses, in the epigraph to this chapter, is fictional transubstantiation: the narrative of the incarnation, the supernatural becoming natural at "the still point of the turning world," to quote the Anglo-Catholic T. S. Eliot in *Four Quartets* ("Burnt Norton"). Therefore, Callaghan's objective metaphors are imbued with divine correlatives and his characters with theological vocation. However, he also shares the potential problematics of Greene, Mauriac, and Flannery O'Connor; attempting to resolve spiritual conflicts within the secular world, he becomes increasingly ambiguous about the manifestation of grace in nature.

As a result of these doctrinal orientations, MacLennan's structures tend to be motivated by theme and Callaghan's by character. Both novelists treat the existential sufferings of their characters with dignity and compassion. But, in their solutions, their respective artistic weaknesses — MacLennan's didacticism and Callaghan's "moral flabbiness" — are the inevitable artistic results of their theological traditions. Although both use a form of "concrete universals" to ground their symbolism, MacLennan's fictional archetypes are more often classical and Callaghan's biblical. In both cases, however, the danger is that these allegorical emblems become either obtrusive or obscure when forced to substitute for clear plotting and characterization. For MacLennan, in *The Watch That Ends the Night* for example, Jerome's canoe and Catherine's rheumatic heart remain hypothetical abstractions, Platonic representations for the crises of the twentieth century. On the other hand, Callaghan's "three stars" for Father Dowling struggle with "the cold smooth waves" (*SB* 287-88) to communicate a clear fictional resolution within the Aristotelian doctrine translated by another Catholic writer as "No ideas but in things" (Hood, "Ontology" 130).

Not surprisingly, mainstream Christian fiction has been relatively rare in Canada in this secular century. There are only two other prominent authors who can be said to have inherited from Callaghan and MacLennan the mantle of the overtly Christian novelist. Interestingly, they also are, respectively, Catholic and Protestant. Their narrative strategies in the present post-modern era, and their respective reputations, are further illustrations of the problematics of faith and fiction in a secular era.

Hugh Hood, by the early 1970s, "had established himself as both a major novelist and one of Canada's finest writers of short stories" (Jackel 56). Much more intentionally and intellectually a Catholic writer than his original mentor, Morley Callaghan, he deliberately redefines fiction in order to convey his fairly orthodox and conservative faith. As he explains in his essays, "The Absolute Infant" and "The Ontology of Super-realism" (his label for his art of "moral realism"), he rejects Platonic dualism for the Aristotelian-Thomist doctrine of the unity and redemption of the world in the Incarnation and "the art that exhibits the transcendental element dwelling in living things" (Hood, "Ontology" 130-31). His novels, while brilliantly detailing the texture, and even trivia, of human existence, are illumined by a "moral imagination" that projects onto "things. . . the colouring [that] has already been put there by the divine act of creation." Therefore, whereas we speculated that MacLennan began his fictions with an idea, and Callaghan with a character, Hood appears to begin his with a thing in which, through a Wordsworthian "visionary gleam," he perceives the divine essence in the immanent, "the noumenal in the phenomenal" ("Ontology" 132-33).

However, this desire to make fiction a "secular analogy to Scripture" has resulted in his increasing rejection of the conventions of modern realistic fiction, "the post-Flaubertian psychological novel of character and incident" ("Letter" 140-41). Instead, he has adopted the Dantean allegorical model of "emblems" to evoke the "essences" of characters and the "epiphanies" of plots. His attempt to demonstrate form in matter results in a technical preoccupation with formal symmetry and genre as a "scaffolding for the imagination" ("Ontology" 128). In his first four novels he explored in turn the parable, the romance, the realistic novel, and the fantasy-satire — all with some success. However, in his *magnum opus, The New Age/Le nouveau siècle* (twelve novels between 1975 and 2000), he has deliberately attempted to assimilate the realistic novel into "the mode of fully-developed Christian allegory" and has refused to be bound by "the forms of ordinary realism" ("Epistolary Conversation" 145). This "documentary fantasy" or "social mythology" ("Interview" 79) unites historical events and fictional characters to demonstrate, within the vast canvas of Canada in the twentieth century, the redemption of Time in Eternity.

The literary reception of this modern Canadian Dante has been mixed and, therefore, illustrative of both the writers' problematics in and the readers' responses to contemporary religious fiction. His first two novels in the ambitious *The New Age* series, *The Swing in the Garden* (1975) and *A New Athens* (1977), were well received, but the volumes since then have elicited increasingly faint praise. Critics have applauded Hood's ambitious scope, his obvious intelligence and sensitivity, his illumination of significant moral form in amazingly detailed and various human matter, and his technical artistry. They have also criticized his (naive?) theological optimism and his allegorization of realism, both of which result in insipid characters, non-dramatic plots, and endless didactic digressions. Perhaps, most significantly, since the mid-1980s critics and readers have increasingly ignored him, and Hood, himself, seems to be writing for a coterie audience.

Hood's very intentional and intellectual solution to the contra-dictions of the modern religious novel is a reapplication of Christian allegory. His sacramental theology redeems life, but its resurrection is a cold pastoral. John Mills has even accused him of Pelagianism ("Epistolary Conversation" 134-35). Certainly, his eternal optimism concerning evil avoids the potential Manichaeism of Callaghan, but it does not adequately engage original sin. Even in *Black and White Keys* (1982), which alternates and juxtaposes the atrocities of Nazi Germany with the innocent pleasures of Toronto during World War II, the blacks are effectively silenced by the whites. As gifted as Hood is (and esteemed as a short-story writer), as a novelist this Catholic has not been able to demonstrate a wholly successful narrative strategy for combining faith and fiction.

A measure of Hugh Hood's marginalization is that Linda Hutcheon omits him entirely from *The Canadian Postmodern: A Study of Contemporary English-Canadian Fiction* (1988). In contrast, she devotes forty-six references to the other mainstream Christian novelist in Canada: Rudy Wiebe, winner of two Governor General's Awards, the latest for his best-selling novel, *A Discovery of Strangers* (1994). Wiebe is clearly an anomaly among successful and respected Canadian novelists; he is a professing Christian, raised in the conservative sect of Mennonite Brethren but forced to resign as editor of the denominational newspaper for his demythologizing of Mennonite history in his first novel, *Peace Shall Destroy Many* (1962).

Wiebe's theology is as intentionally ideological as Hood's, but it is expressed in a typically Mennonite concern for social justice. Wiebe was deeply influenced by the theologian John Howard Yoder whom he encountered at Goshen College, Indiana: "[Yoder's] best book is *The*

Politics of Jesus which takes apart the social situation in which Jesus lived to prove the alternatives Jesus had and why he chose to act the way he did when he could have done other kinds of things" (qtd. in Neuman 243). Wiebe translates what Christianity calls "The Great Commission" into the artist's responsibility to be "both critic and witness" to society through his art. But "the novel is not a systematic theology"; it is a work of art that shows "man as he is" and "what man by God's grace may become" ("The Artist" 42-47).

This radical Christian mission within a non-Christian world is expressed in his first three novels. The first portrays the tensions within a conservative, pacifist Mennonite community caused by the influences of the larger secular and violent world during World War II. *First and Vital Candle* (1966) less successfully portrays the protagonist's struggle between his lost faith and the corruption of the faithless world.

The Blue Mountains of China (1970), however, established his competence and reputation in the epic mode which has become his fictional trademark. It is a brilliant "historiographic metafiction" (Hutcheon 210) — a post-modern, polyphonic, deconstruction of historical myth on a vast scale. Like his later epics about aboriginal peoples, *The Blue Mountains of China* also explores the community and spirituality of a marginalized people. It covers one hundred years of Mennonite history on four continents and traces the diaspora of Russian Mennonites to Canada, China, and Paraguay through four families, nine narrative voices, and an intricate structure crisscrossing time and space. The Mennonite pilgrimage to freedom is a metaphor for the modern, universal quest for meaning; it realistically explores the relative options of Christian faith and secular materialism through an apparent (if debatable) dialogic structure (Van Toorn 69). The novel's conclusion, however, demonstrates the problems of imposing theological closure on fictional flux. In the final chapter, the polyphonic medley of voices changes into a univocal sermon by Wiebe's spokesperson, John Reimer. He deconstructs the Mennonite isolationist myth of the Promised Land (symbolized in the title) and substitutes a theology of social responsibility: "[Jesus] was alive, on earth to lead a revolution. . . for social justice" (215).

In *The Temptations of Big Bear* (1973), *The Scorched-Wood People* (1977), and *A Discovery of Strangers* (1994), Wiebe similarly creates epic historiographic metafictions which challenge authoritative texts with oral traditions. In these novels he combines religion with his other main influence, his roots in the Canadian West, and he interrogates the eurocentric conceptions of both in his portrayals of the conflicts between whites and aboriginals. He depicts Big Bear as the Cree chief who defies the European linear partitioning of the prairies with his animistic devotion to the land. The Métis "Prophet," Louis Riel, gives vision and voice to his "scorched-wood people" and is crucified by white political power and

capitalistic corruption.   In *A Discovery of Strangers* the spiritual
inclusiveness of the Dene people with the land is contrasted with the
ecological destruction and cultural elitism of the Englishmen in the Franklin
Expedition.   These historical revisions self-consciously subvert European
religious creeds of reason and progress through a native religious revelation
of the fallibility of texts and the immutability of the spirit.

Wiebe's post-colonial politics and post-modern texts have earned
him critical acclaim in Canada and abroad, despite some reservations
concerning his "difficult" style (Keith 12), moral didacticism, and overt
spirituality. We might speculate that his relative success in combining faith
and fiction (compared to the logocentricity of MacLennan and the
sacramentalism of Callaghan and Hood) owes less to the Protestant
theology of his faith and more to the post-modern redefinition of reality in
his fiction. While traditional religious novelists may attempt to imbue
nature with the supernatural in realistic texts, Wiebe apparently interrogates
the concept of both transparent and transcendental realism in his
"metafictional" and "metaphorical" narratives (Hutcheon 54-55). Accepting
the novel's construction, rather than reflection (mimesis) of reality, Wiebe
then foregrounds his theological assumptions in his self-reflexive version of
history. Thus, he avoids the modern incredulity toward the spiritual in the
secular (the central problem for the modern religious novel) by inviting his
readers themselves to mediate between the spiritual text and their secular
lives.

Throughout this volume we have analysed the problem of the
modern religious novel — the paradox of a traditional spiritual faith in a
modern secular world. As we have seen, T. R. Wright has argued that the
realistic novel is a construct of ideological empiricism (110).   Therefore,
many twentieth century religious writers, including MacLennan and
Callaghan, have variously attempted to redefine their faith to accommodate
realistic fiction. But what if, conversely, "reality" is a construct of fiction?
Hugh Hood and Rudy Wiebe have, apparently, accepted this post-modern
concept in their attempts to redefine their fiction rather than their faith. I
suggest, however, that Hood's narrative strategy is ultimately regressive in
his attempt to refigure medieval Christian allegory in modern dress. It is,
rather, Wiebe's post-colonial ideology of social justice and his post-modern
genre of historiographic metafiction that may be the contemporary narrative
answer to the theological vocation of expressing faith in fiction.

WORKS CITED

Adams, James Luther. *Paul Tillich's Philosophy of Culture, Science and Religion.* New York: Harper and Row, 1965.

Bandy, Thomas G. "Tillich's Limited Understanding of the Thought of Henri Bergson as 'Life Philosophy'." *Theonomy and Autonomy: Studies in Paul Tillich's Engagement with Modern Culture.* Ed. John J. Carey. Macon, GA: Mercer University Press, 1984. 3-17.

Bartlett, Donald R. "Callaghan's Troubled (and Troubling) Heroines." *University of Windsor Review* 16.1 (1981): 60-72.

Boire, Gary. "Morley Callaghan and His Works." *Canadian Writers and Their Works.* Ed. Robert Lecker, Jack David, and Ellen Quigley. Fiction Series 5. Toronto: ECW Press, 1990.

_____. *Morley Callaghan: Literary Anarchist.* Toronto: ECW Press, 1994.

Booth, Wayne C. *The Rhetoric of Fiction.* Chicago: University of Chicago Press, 1961.

Callaghan, Morley. *A Broken Journey.* New York: Scribner's, 1932.

_____ "A Christmas Meditation on Faith, Hope and Charity." *Chatelaine* December. 1983: 61,102,106.

_____. *Close to the Sun Again.* Toronto: Macmillan, 1977.

_____. "An excerpt from Morley Callaghan's speech of acceptance on receiving the Royal Bank Award, June 15, 1970." *Sixteen by Twelve.* Ed. John Metcalf. Toronto: Ryerson, 1970. 20-21.

_____. *A Fine and Private Place.* Toronto: Macmillan, 1975.

_____. "Interview." *Quill and Quire.* July 1983: 17.

_____. *It's Never Over.* New York: Scribner's, 1930.

_____. *The Loved and the Lost.* Toronto: Macmillan, 1951.

_____. *Luke Baldwin's Vow.* Toronto: Winston, 1948.

_____. "The Man with the Coat." *Maclean's Magazine* April 1955: 11-19, 81-94, 100-19.

_____. *The Many Colored Coat.* Toronto: Macmillan, 1960.

_____. *More Joy in Heaven.* New York: Random House, 1937.

_____. *Morley Callaghan's Stories.* Toronto: Macmillan, 1959.

_____. *A Native Argosy.* New York: Scribner's, 1929.

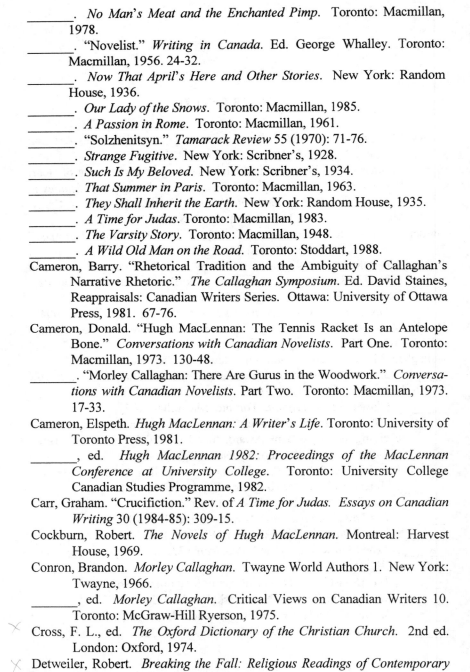
_____. *No Man's Meat and the Enchanted Pimp*. Toronto: Macmillan, 1978.

_____. "Novelist." *Writing in Canada*. Ed. George Whalley. Toronto: Macmillan, 1956. 24-32.

_____. *Now That April's Here and Other Stories*. New York: Random House, 1936.

_____. *Our Lady of the Snows*. Toronto: Macmillan, 1985.

_____. *A Passion in Rome*. Toronto: Macmillan, 1961.

_____. "Solzhenitsyn." *Tamarack Review* 55 (1970): 71-76.

_____. *Strange Fugitive*. New York: Scribner's, 1928.

_____. *Such Is My Beloved*. New York: Scribner's, 1934.

_____. *That Summer in Paris*. Toronto: Macmillan, 1963.

_____. *They Shall Inherit the Earth*. New York: Random House, 1935.

_____. *A Time for Judas*. Toronto: Macmillan, 1983.

_____. *The Varsity Story*. Toronto: Macmillan, 1948.

_____. *A Wild Old Man on the Road*. Toronto: Stoddart, 1988.

Cameron, Barry. "Rhetorical Tradition and the Ambiguity of Callaghan's Narrative Rhetoric." *The Callaghan Symposium*. Ed. David Staines, Reappraisals: Canadian Writers Series. Ottawa: University of Ottawa Press, 1981. 67-76.

Cameron, Donald. "Hugh MacLennan: The Tennis Racket Is an Antelope Bone." *Conversations with Canadian Novelists*. Part One. Toronto: Macmillan, 1973. 130-48.

_____. "Morley Callaghan: There Are Gurus in the Woodwork." *Conversations with Canadian Novelists*. Part Two. Toronto: Macmillan, 1973. 17-33.

Cameron, Elspeth. *Hugh MacLennan: A Writer's Life*. Toronto: University of Toronto Press, 1981.

_____, ed. *Hugh MacLennan 1982: Proceedings of the MacLennan Conference at University College*. Toronto: University College Canadian Studies Programme, 1982.

Carr, Graham. "Crucifiction." Rev. of *A Time for Judas*. *Essays on Canadian Writing* 30 (1984-85): 309-15.

Cockburn, Robert. *The Novels of Hugh MacLennan*. Montreal: Harvest House, 1969.

Conron, Brandon. *Morley Callaghan*. Twayne World Authors 1. New York: Twayne, 1966.

_____, ed. *Morley Callaghan*. Critical Views on Canadian Writers 10. Toronto: McGraw-Hill Ryerson, 1975.

Cross, F. L., ed. *The Oxford Dictionary of the Christian Church*. 2nd ed. London: Oxford, 1974.

Detweiler, Robert. *Breaking the Fall: Religious Readings of Contemporary Fiction*. London: Macmillan, 1989.

Dooley, D. J. "Catching Up with Theology." *Queen's Quarterly* 75 (1968): 247-60.

———. "*Each Man's Son*: The Daemon of Hope and Imagination." *Journal of Canadian Studies* 14.4 (1979-80): 66-75.

———. "Love and Betrayal." Rev. of *A Time for Judas. Canadian Forum* October 1983. 24-25.

———. *Moral Vision in the Canadian Novel.* Toronto: Clarke, Irwin, 1979.

Dunaway, John M. *Jacques Maritain.* Twayne World Authors 474. Boston: Twayne, 1978.

Dunn, William. "Morley Callaghan." *Dictionary of Literary Biography.* Vol. 68. Ed. W. H. New. Detroit: Gale, 1988. 42-54.

Eliot, T. S. *Four Quartets.* London: Faber and Faber, 1944.

———. *On Poetry and Poets.* London: Faber and Faber, 1957.

Ferris, Ina. "Morley Callaghan and the Exultant Self." *Journal of Canadian Studies* 15.1 (1980):13-17.

Fetherling, Douglas. "The Gospel Without the Preaching." *Maclean's* 19 September 1983:14,16.

Gibson, Douglas, ed. *Hugh MacLennan's Best.* Toronto: McClelland and Stewart, 1991.

Glicksberg, Charles I. *Modern Literature and the Death of God.* The Hague: Martinus Nijhoff, 1966.

Goetsch, Paul. "Too Long to the Courtly Muses: Hugh MacLennan as a Contemporary Writer." *Canadian Literature* 10 (1961): 19-31.

Grant, John Webster. "'At Least You Knew Where You Stood with Them': Reflections on Religious Pluralism in Canada and the United States." *Studies in Religion* 2 (1973): 340-51.

Greene, Graham. *The Heart of the Matter.* 1948. Harmondsworth: Penguin, 1971.

Gunn, Giles. *The Interpretation of Otherness: Literature, Religion, and the American Imagination.* New York: Oxford, 1979.

Hanna, Thomas L. "A Question: What Does One Mean by 'Religious Literature'?" Panichas 74-86.

Hawkins, Peter S. *The Language of Grace: Flannery O'Connor, Walker Percy, and Iris Murdoch.* New Haven: Cowley, 1983.

Hood, Hugh. *Be Sure to Close Your Eyes.* The New Age 9. Toronto: Anansi, 1993.

———. *Black and White Keys.* The New Age 4. Toronto: ECW Press, 1982.

———. *The Camera Always Lies.* New York: Harcourt, Brace and World, 1967.

———. *Dead Men's Watches.* The New Age 10. Toronto: Anansi, 1995.

———. *A Game of Touch.* Don Mills: Longman, 1970.

_____. "An Interview with Hugh Hood." *Hugh Hood's Work in Progress.*
Ed. J. R. (Tim) Struthers. *Essays on Canadian Writing* 13/14
(1978-79): 21-93.

_____. "Letter." *Essays on Canadian Writing.* 9 (1977-78): 139-41.

_____. *The Motor Boys in Ottawa.* The New Age 6. Toronto: Stoddart,
1986.

_____. *A New Athens.* The New Age 2. Ottawa: Oberon, 1977.

_____. "The Ontology of Super-realism" and "The Absolute Infant." *The
Governor's Bridge Is Closed.* Ottawa: Oberon, 1973. 126-35; 136-44.

_____. *Property and Value.* The New Age 8. Toronto: Anansi, 1990.

_____. *Reservoir Ravine.* The New Age 3. Ottawa: Oberon, 1979.

_____. *The Scenic Art.* The New Age 5. Toronto: Stoddart, 1984.

_____. *The Swing in the Garden.* The New Age 1. Ottawa: Oberon, 1975.

_____. *Tony's Book.* The New Age 7. Toronto: Stoddart, 1988.

_____. *White Figure, White Ground.* Toronto: Ryerson, 1964.

_____. *You Can't Get There from Here.* Ottawa: Oberon, 1972.

_____ and John Mills. "Hugh Hood and John Mills in Epistolary
Conversation." *Fiddlehead* 116 (1978): 133-46.

Hoy, Helen. "Hugh MacLennan and His Works." *Canadian Writers and
Their Works.* Ed. Robert Lecker, Jack David and Ellen Quigley.
Fiction Series 5. Toronto: ECW Press, 1990. 149-212.

_____. Rev. of *A Time for Judas. University of Toronto Quarterly* 53.4 (1984):
329.

Hutcheon, Linda. *The Canadian Postmodern: A Study of Contemporary
English-Canadian Fiction.* Toronto: Oxford University Press, 1988.

Hyman, Roger. "Too Many Voices; Too Many Times: Hugh MacLennan's
Unfulfilled Ambitions." *Queen's Quarterly* 89.2 (1982): 313-24.

Jackel, David. "Short Fiction." *Literary History of: Canadian Literature in
English.* Ed. W. H. New. 2nd ed. Vol. 4. Toronto: University of
Toronto Press, 1990. 46-72.

James, William. *The Varieties of Religious Experience.* 1902. London:
Fontana-Collins, 1960.

Keith, W. J. *Epic Fiction: The Art of Rudy Wiebe.* Edmonton: University of
Alberta Press, 1981.

Kendle, Judith. "Tragic or Romantic Vision." Rev. of *Close to the Sun Again.
Journal of Canadian Fiction* 24 (1979): 141-44.

Klinck, Carl F., ed. *Literary History of Canada: Canadian Literature in
English.* Toronto: University of Toronto Press, 1965.

Krieger, Murray. *The Tragic Vision: Variations on a Theme in Literary
Interpretation.* Chicago: Phoenix-University of Chicago Press, 1966.

Leith, Linda. *Introducing Hugh MacLennan's "Two Solitudes."* Toronto:
ECW Press, 1990.

Lucas, Alec. *Hugh MacLennan.* New Canadian Library. Canadian Writers 8. Toronto: McClelland and Stewart, 1970.

MacLennan, Hugh. *Barometer Rising.* New York: Duell, Sloan and Pearce, 1941.

⸻. *The Colour of Canada.* Toronto: McClelland and Stewart, 1967.

⸻. *Cross-Country.* 1949. Edmonton: Hurtig, 1972.

⸻. "The Defence of *Lady Chatterley.*" *Canadian Literature* 6 (1960): 18-23.

⸻. *Each Man's Son.* Toronto: Macmillan, 1951.

⸻. *The Other Side of Hugh MacLennan: Essays Old and New.* Ed. Elspeth Cameron. Toronto: Macmillan, 1978.

⸻. *The Precipice.* Toronto: Collins, 1948.

⸻. "Quebec Crisis Bares the Agony of Youth." *Toronto Telegram.* Toronto 21 November 1970: 17+.

⸻. "Reflections on Two Decades." *Canadian Literature* 41(1969): 28-39.

⸻. *Return of the Sphinx.* Toronto: Macmillan, 1967.

⸻. *Scotchman's Return and Other Essays.* Toronto: Macmillan, 1960.

⸻. *Seven Rivers of Canada: The MacKenzie, the St. Lawrence, the Ottawa, the Red, the Saskatchewan, the Fraser, the St. John.* Toronto: Macmillan, 1961.

⸻. "The Story of a Novel." *Canadian Literature* 3 (1960): 35-39. Rpt. in Smith 33-38.

⸻. *Thirty and Three.* Ed. Dorothy Duncan. Toronto: Macmillan, 1954.

⸻. *Two Solitudes.* Toronto: Collins, 1945.

⸻. *Voices in Time.* Toronto: Macmillan, 1980.

⸻. *The Watch That Ends the Night.* Toronto: Macmillan, 1959.

MacLulich, T. D. *Between Europe and America: The Canadian Tradition in Fiction.* Toronto: ECW Press, 1988.

Maritain, Jacques. *Art and Scholasticism with Other Essays.* Trans. J. F. Scanlan. London: Sheed and Ward, 1934.

⸻. *Existence and the Existent.* Trans. Lewis Galantiere and Gerald B. Phelan. New York: Random House, 1948.

⸻. *Integral Humanism: Temporal and Spiritual Problems of a New Christendom.* Trans. Joseph W. Evans. New York: Scribner's, 1968.

⸻. *Range of Reason.* New York: Scribner's, 1952.

Marshall, Joyce. "Morley Callaghan 1903-1990: A Tribute." *Books in Canada* October 1990: 11-12.

Mathews, Robin. "Hugh MacLennan: The Nationalist Dilemma in Canada." *Studies in Canadian Literature* 1.1 (1976): 49-63.

_____. "Ideology, Class and Literary Structure: A Basis for Criticism of Hugh MacLennan's Novels." E. Cameron, *Hugh MacLennan 1982* 69-83.

_____. "The Night That Ends the Debauch." *Books in Canada.* August-September 1980: 4-6.

McPherson, Hugo. "The Two Worlds of Morley Callaghan." *Queen's Quarterly* 44 (1957): 350-65. Rpt. in Conron, Critical Views 60-73.

Morley, Patricia. "Callaghan's Vision: Wholeness and the Individual." *Journal of Canadian Studies* 15.1 (1980): 8-12.

Neuman, Shirley. "Unearthing Language: An Interview with Rudy Wiebe and Robert Kroetsch." *A Voice in the Land: Essays By and About Rudy Wiebe.* Ed. W. J. Keith. Edmonton: NeWest, 1981. 226-47.

New, W. H. *A History of Canadian Literature.* London: Macmillan, 1989.

O'Connor, Flannery. *Mystery and Manners.* Eds. S. Fitzgerald and R. Fitzgerald. New York: Farrar, Straus, and Giroux, 1969.

O'Connor, John. "Fraternal Twins: The Impact of Jacques Maritain on Callaghan and Charbonneau." *Mosaic* 14.2 (1981): 145-63.

Pacey, Desmond. *Creative Writing in Canada.* 2nd ed. Toronto: McGraw-Hill Ryerson, 1967.

_____. "Fiction (1920-1940)." Klinck 658-93.

Panichas, George, A., ed. *Mansions of the Spirit: Essays in Literature and Religion.* New York: Hawthorn, 1967.

Reinhardt, Kurt F. *The Theological Novel of Modern Europe: An Analysis of Masterpieces by Eight Authors.* New York: Frederick Ungar, 1969.

Roper, Gordon, Rupert Schieder, and S. Ross Beharriell. "The Kinds of Fiction (1880-1920)." Klinck 284-312.

Ross, Malcolm. Introduction. *Such Is My Beloved.* By Morley Callaghan. New Canadian Library. Toronto: McClelland and Stewart, 1957.

Smith, A. J. M., ed. *Masks of Fiction: Canadian Critics on Canadian Prose.* New Canadian Library. Toronto: McClelland and Stewart, 1961.

Staines, David. "Commentary on W. J. Keith." E. Cameron, *Hugh MacLennan 1982* 64-68.

_____. "Morley Callaghan: The Writer and His Writings." *The Callaghan Symposium.* Ed. David Staines. Reappraisals: Canadian Writers Series. Ottawa: University of Ottawa Press, 1981. 111-21.

Stratford, Philip. *Faith and Fiction: Creative Process in Greene and Mauriac.* Notre Dame: University of Notre Dame Press, 1964.

Tennyson, G. B., and Edward E. Ericson, Jr., eds. *Religion and Modern Literature: Essays in Theory and Criticism.* Grand Rapids: Eerdmans, 1975.

Tillich, Paul. *The Courage to Be.* 1952. London: Fontana-Collins, 1962.

_____. *Perspectives on 19th and 20th Century Protestant Theology.* Ed. Carl E. Braaten. New York: Harper and Row, 1967.

_____. *Theology of Culture*. Ed. Robert C. Kimball. 1959. New York: Galaxy-Oxford, 1964.

Twigg, Alan. "Hugh MacLennan: Patricius." *For Openers: Conversations with 24 Canadian Writers*. Madeira Park, B.C.: Harbour, 1981. 83-96.

Van Toorn, Penny. *Rudy Wiebe and the Historicity of the Word*. Edmonton: University of Alberta Press, 1995.

Watt, F. W. "Letters in Canada: 1961: Fiction." Rev. of *A Passion in Rome*, by Morley Callaghan. *University of Toronto Quarterly* 31 (1962): 455-57.

_____. "Morley Callaghan as Thinker." *Dalhousie Review* 39 (1959): 305-13. Rpt. in Smith 116-27.

_____. "Morley Callaghan's *A Passion in Rome*." *Varsity Graduate* 9.5 (1962): 6-12. Rpt. in Conron, Critical Views 84-87.

Weaver, Robert. "A Talk with Morley Callaghan." *Tamarack Review* 7 (1958): 3-29.

Wicker, Brian. *The Story-Shaped World: Fiction and Metaphysics: Some Variations on a Theme*. London: Athlone Press, 1975.

Wiebe, Rudy. "The Artist as a Critic and a Witness." *A Voice in the Land: Essays By and About Rudy Wiebe* Ed. W. J. Keith. Edmonton: NeWest, 1981. 39-47.

_____. *The Blue Mountains of China*. Toronto: McClelland and Stewart, 1970.

_____. *A Discovery of Strangers*. Toronto: Knopf, 1994.

_____. *First and Vital Candle*. Toronto: McClelland and Stewart, 1966.

_____. *Peace Shall Destroy Many*. Toronto: McClelland and Stewart, 1962.

_____. *The Scorched-Wood People*. Toronto: McClelland and Stewart, 1977.

_____. *The Temptations of Big Bear*. Toronto: McClelland and Stewart, 1973.

Wilder, Amos. *Theology and Modern Literature*. Cambridge: Harvard University Press, 1967.

Wilson, Edmund. "Morley Callaghan of Toronto." *O Canada: An American's Notes on Canadian Culture*. New York: Farrar, 1964. 9-31. Rpt. in Conron, Critical Views 106-19.

Wilson, Milton. "Callaghan's Caviare." *Tamarack Review* 22 (1962): 88-93. Rpt. in Conron, Critical Views 79-83.

Woodcock, George. *Hugh MacLennan*. Studies in Canadian Literature 5. Toronto: Copp Clark, 1969.

_____. *Introducing Hugh MacLennan's "Barometer Rising": A Reader's Guide*. ECW Press, 1989.

_____. "Lost Eurydice: The Novels of Callaghan." *Canadian Literature* 21 (1964): 21-35. Rpt. in Conron, Critical Views 88-103.

Wright, T. R. *Theology and Literature*. Oxford: Blackwell, 1988.

INDEX

139

Series Published by Wilfrid Laurier University Press for the Canadian Corporation for Studies in Religion / Corporation Canadienne des Sciences Religieuses

Editions SR

1. *La langue de Ya'udi : description et classement de l'ancien parler de Zencircli dans le cadre des langues sémitiques du nord-ouest*
   Paul-Eugène Dion, O.P. / 1974 / viii + 511 p. / OUT OF PRINT
2. *The Conception of Punishment in Early Indian Literature*
   Terence P. Day / 1982 / iv + 328 pp.
3. *Traditions in Contact and Change: Selected Proceedings of the XIVth Congress of the International Association for the History of Religions*
   Edited by Peter Slater and Donald Wiebe with Maurice Boutin and Harold Coward
   1983 / x + 758 pp. / OUT OF PRINT
4. *Le messianisme de Louis Riel*
   Gilles Martel / 1984 / xviii + 483 p.
5. *Mythologies and Philosophies of Salvation in the Theistic Traditions of India*
   Klaus K. Klostermaier / 1984 / xvi + 549 pp. / OUT OF PRINT
6. *Averroes' Doctrine of Immortality: A Matter of Controversy*
   Ovey N. Mohammed / 1984 / vi + 202 pp. / OUT OF PRINT
7. *L'étude des religions dans les écoles : l'expérience américaine, anglaise et canadienne*
   Fernand Ouellet / 1985 / xvi + 666 pp.
8. *Of God and Maxim Guns: Presbyterianism in Nigeria, 1846-1966*
   Geoffrey Johnston / 1988 / iv + 322 pp.
9. *A Victorian Missionary and Canadian Indian Policy: Cultural Synthesis vs Cultural Replacement*
   David A. Nock / 1988 / x + 194 pp. / OUT OF PRINT
10. *Prometheus Rebound: The Irony of Atheism*
    Joseph C. McLelland / 1988 / xvi + 366 pp.
11. *Competition in Religious Life*
    Jay Newman / 1989 / viii + 237 pp.
12. *The Huguenots and French Opinion, 1685-1787: The Enlightenment Debate on Toleration*
    Geoffrey Adams / 1991 / xiv + 335 pp.
13. *Religion in History: The Word, the Idea, the Reality / La religion dans l'histoire : le mot, l'idée, la réalité*
    Edited by/Sous la direction de Michel Despland and/et Gérard Vallée
    1992 / x + 252 pp.
14. *Sharing Without Reckoning: Imperfect Right and the Norms of Reciprocity*
    Millard Schumaker / 1992 / xiv + 112 pp.
15. *Love and the Soul: Psychological Interpretations of the Eros and Psyche Myth*
    James Gollnick / 1992 / viii + 174 pp.
16. *The Promise of Critical Theology: Essays in Honour of Charles Davis*
    Edited by Marc P. Lalonde / 1995 / xii + 146 pp.
17. *The Five Aggregates: Understanding Theravāda Psychology and Soteriology*
    Mathieu Boisvert / 1995 / xii + 166 pp.
18. *Mysticism and Vocation*
    James R. Horne / 1996 / vi + 110 pp.
19. *Memory and Hope: Strands of Canadian Baptist History*
    Edited by David T. Priestley / 1996 / viii + 211 pp.

Comparative Ethics Series / Collection d'Éthique Comparée

Dissertations SR

Studies in Christianity and Judaism / Études sur le christianisme et le judaïsme

The Study of Religion in Canada /
Sciences Religieuses au Canada

Studies in Women and Religion /
Études sur les femmes et la religion

SR Supplements

Available from:

WILFRID LAURIER UNIVERSITY PRESS

Waterloo, Ontario, Canada   N2L 3C5
Telephone: (519) 884-0710, ext. 6124
Fax: (519) 725-1399
E-mail: press@mach1.wlu.ca
World Wide Web: http://info.wlu.ca/~wwwpress